Murder, Mayhem, and Moonshine:
True Macon County Crime Stories

By CL Gammon

Deep Read Press

www.deepreadpress.com

615-670-1725

LAFAYETTE, TENNESSEE
deepreadpress@gmail.com

Text Copyright © 2022 by CL Gammon

Cover Design © 2022 by Kim Gammon

All Rights Reserved.

No part of this book may be reproduced, scanned, or distributed in any printed or electronic form without permission of the publisher, except as part of a literary review.

Please do not participate in or encourage piracy of copyrighted materials in violation of the author's rights. Purchase only authorized editions.

The publisher does not have any control over, and does not assume any responsibility for, author or third-party websites or their content.

The publisher offers discounts for bulk purchases. Please contact the publisher at the email address below for details.

First Deep Read Press Edition

Manufactured in the United States of America

ISBN: 978-1-954989-25-2 (Paperback)

ISBN: 978-1-954989-26-9 (Hardback)

Edited by Kim Gammon

Cover Design by: Kim Gammon

Published by:

DEEP READ PRESS

Lafayette, Tennessee

www.deepreadpress.com

deepreadpress@gmail.com

Murder, Mayhem, and Moonshine

For the good folk of Macon County

CL Gammon's Other Local History Titles

Murder, Mayhem, and Moonshine: True Macon County Crime Stories is CL Gammon's eleventh local history title. The others are:

Ballyhoo: John Butler and the Monkey Trial

Bizarre Tales from Macon County

Blood on the Cumberland: The Battle of Hartsville

Death on the Highland: Spanish Flu in Macon County

Dixie Witches: 9 True Southern Witch Trials

Hanging the Macon County Witch

Revenue Raiders: Macon County's Whiskey War

Shallow Graves and Shattered Dreams: Solving the Murders of Three Macon County Men

The Macon County Race War

You can find them all on www.amazon.com, or you can email the publisher, Deep Read Press, at deepreadpress@gmail.com and arrange for direct purchase.

Table of Contents

Introduction	Page 9
1. Murder on the Square	Page 11
2. Wildcatters Shoot Deputy	Page 28
3. Deputy Murdered	Page 31
4. Deputy Marshal Wounded	Page 35
5. Murder at Eulia Church	Page 37
6. Fracas at a Circus	Page 39
7. A Child Abduction	Page 41
8. Disrupted Church Services	Page 43
9. Shootout Kills Horse	Page 45
10. A Mail Robbery	Page 46
11. Rapist on the Loose	Page 49
12. Court Charges Forty-Seven	Page 51
13. A Blackmail Plot	Page 53
14. Bullying Leads to Killing	Page 55
15. Wife Beater Slain	Page 57
16. A Vicious Assault	Page 59
17. Landlord Shot Down	Page 63
18. Fugitive Found	Page 65
19. A Horse Rustling Ring	Page 67
20. Dead Man Robs Post Office	Page 69
21. Obnoxious Man Beaten	Page 75

Murder, Mayhem, and Moonshine

22. Stray Bullet Injures Horse	Page 77
23. Shootout as Social Event	Page 79
24. A $5 Bribe Offer	Page 80
25. Three Killed at Dance	Page 83
26. Illegal Telephone Service?	Page 85
27. A Fowl Dispute and a Killing	Page 88
28. An Unhappy Record	Page 90
29. Macon Sheriff Arrested	Page 92
30. Henry Crook Kills Again	Page 94
31. Man Mistaken for Bear	Page 96
32. Murder on the Square, Again	Page 99
33. A Bail Jumper Kidnapped	Page 103
34. Murder at Highland School	Page 105
35. The Cigar Wrapper Shooting	Page 111
36. Murder at the County Fair	Page 112
37. A Commie in Macon County	Page 119
38. A Draft Dodger?	Page 125
39. Hanes Busts up Stills	Page 127
40. The Macon County Dog Tax	Page 129
41. Deputy Kills Prisoner	Page 131
42. Trusting Sheriff Tricked	Page 134
43. A Dedicated Revenue Agent	Page 136
44. Sheriff Frye Gunned Down	Page 139
45. Posse Pursues Thieves	Page 143
46. The Bloody Truck Mystery	Page 145

47. Man Kills In-Law	Page 148
48. Speeder Disrupts Egg Hunt	Page 150
49. Young Bank Robbers	Page 152
50. Jackson County Raid	Page 156
51. A Clever Counterfeiter	Page 158
52. Driving Legally	Page 161
53. The Willie Holland Murder	Page 165
54. The Stolen Smokes Shooting	Page 168
55. Bloodhounds at Webbtown	Page 170
56. The Courthouse Arson Case	Page 172
57. Vance General Store Robbed	Page 190
58. Man Killed with Hoe	Page 194
59. A Home Invasion	Page 197
60. Glover Accuses Likens	Page 199
61. Murder on Gravel Hill	Page 201
62. Gypsies in Macon County?	Page 206
63. A Nighttime Burglary	Page 209
64. An Accidental Shooting	Page 212
65. Burglars Rob Store	Page 214
66. The Underwood Church Fire	Page 216
67. Rumrunners Shoot Sheriff	Page 218
68. Liquor Raids Continue	Page 223
69. Gangsters in Macon County?	Page 225
70. Another Whiskey Bust	Page 229
71. Civil War Veteran Robbed	Page 231

72. Doctor's Residence Bombed	Page 233
73. Christmas Eve Murder	Page 235
74. Man Killed with Stilt	Page 238
75. Gravel Hill Church Fire	Page 241
Conclusion	Page 243
Acknowledgements	Page 244
About The Author	Page 246
Index	Page 247

Introduction

MACON County, Tennessee is a great place to grow up and it is a great place to live. That is why so many natives, after various sojourns, return home to Macon County to settle down.

Macon County is now, and always has been, a safe place to live when compared to other locales. But no place, not even Macon County, is crime free. This volume relates 75 true crime stories from Macon County between 1879 and 1939.

These stories run the gamut of crime. Some are tragic, some bizarre, some grotesque, and some are a little humorous. Yet, they are all true and the author presents a list of references for each of them.

In some of the cases mentioned here, juries acquitted the accused. In other cases, there was not enough evidence to proceed against the alleged criminals. There is no effort made to editorialize about the judgment of the juries or prosecutors in any of these cases.

Not all these stories describe events that took place in Macon County proper, but all have a direct connection to Macon County.

Although all of the alleged crimes mentioned here took place decades ago, many of them detail the types of crimes that remain common today across the United States and the world. Besides murder, there are stories about child abduction, rape, bullying, domestic violence, racial problems, drunk driving, confidence games, and others.

The hope is that the reader will gain a little greater insight about Macon County and the United States from this book.

Some Notes about the Text.

The information related here comes from newspapers, books, death certificates, and other sources. Sadly, in years gone by, the recording of names and addresses, even on official documents, was often haphazard. Despite the pains taken to verify and list the correct spellings of them all, it is impossible to guarantee the accurate spelling of some of the names listed here.

Another issue is the listing of titles. The titles Justice of the Peace, Squire, and Magistrate, relate to the same office and past writers listed them interchangeably. This book uses the term Justice of the Peace in all cases to prevent confusion. The titles Chairman of the Macon County Court, and Macon County Judge, did not actually signify the same office. The Macon County Judge replaced the Chairman of the Macon County Court, but the term County Judge was in common usage even before the change took place officially. There has been no attempt to change quotes regardless of which term the speaker used.

1. Murder on the Square

WE tend to imagine murder as a modern-day malady – it isn't. Since Cain struck down Abel, the affliction of murder has plagued humanity. Perhaps murder was once less prevalent than it is now, but it has always been with us.

Macon County, Tennessee has always been a safe place to live when compared to other communities, but it has never been a stranger to murder.

This chapter details a notorious murder that took place in front of several eyewitnesses on the Public Square in Lafayette, Tennessee. It also details the legal wrangling of the accused to avoid going to the gallows for his crime, followed by his attempts to avoid punishment altogether. It then relates how the murderer ultimately reaped what he had sown.

The Murder of Hugh Sanders

While many happy events have taken place on the Lafayette Public Square, it has been the site of a number of tragedies as well. One such tragedy took place in 1880.

This story begins when the folk at the Church of Christ located on Lafayette's Public Square (where Macon Bank & Trust is now) reported the theft of a demijohn containing wine they had stored there for use during religious services.

A demijohn is a large, narrow-necked bottle used to hold liquid, especially wine. It is uncertain how much wine the stolen bottle contained, but demijohns usually hold between 1 and 16 gallons.

Though he was only 24-years-old, Joseph Cartwright already had the reputation in the community of being a notorious drunkard. Cartwright came under suspicion for the theft immediately. When questioned about the crime, Cartwright denied any knowledge of the missing wine.

The authorities had little but suspicion and a small bit of circumstantial evidence bolstered by a few dubious witnesses. Despite his skimpy evidence, the District Attorney General became convinced that Cartwright was guilty. The prosecutor plowed ahead and secured an indictment against Cartwright in January 1879.

Joe Cartwright stood trial in April 1879 and a jury acquitted him. Though not convicted, the trial was hard on Joe and his family. His wife Martha Adeline *Brawner* Cartwright was pregnant with their second child (John Wesley Cartwright, born on July 29, 1879) and the fear of her husband going to prison took a toll on her.

A young man not too much different in age from Joe Cartwright named Hugh Sanders testified for the prosecution at Cartwright's trial. This led to hard feelings between the two young men. Cartwright lived within the city limits and Sanders only lived a mile or two outside of Lafayette. The two had many opportunities to see one another and this only fueled their feud. Additionally, the bad blood between Cartwright and Sanders became common knowledge and the whispered rumors it generated did not help matters any.

The animosity between the two young men apparently caused Cartwright to leave Macon County for a short time between his trial for stealing the wine and the homicide of Hugh Sanders. Cartwright's family contended that Joe feared Sanders and that is why he abandoned the county for a few days. Others contested that statement and claimed that he left for other reasons.

Whatever the reason Cartwright left town, and whether or not he feared Sanders, the bad blood between the two men is indisputable. Sanders made threats against Cartwright in front of witnesses numerous times.

Al least once, Hugh Sanders even threatened Cartwright to his face. Sometime between the 3rd and 6th of October, 1880, Sanders came upon Cartwright at a fresh water spring where persons often stopped to refresh themselves from the clear, cold water trickling up from below the surface of the earth.

When Sanders saw Cartwright, he began to act in a provocative manner. Sanders abused Cartwright verbally and one witness said that he was certain that Sanders was about to draw his knife and stab Cartwright. For whatever reason, Sanders left his knife sheaved, but he did make an ominous threat. He promised Cartwright that he would see him again.

It was shortly after Sanders threatened him personally, that Cartwright took leave of the county for a few days.

Apparently, Sanders feared that Cartwright would name him as one of those involved in stealing the wine from the church. When he got wind of rumors that Cartwright intended to implicate him in the robbery, it enraged Sanders. Witnesses swore that Sanders said he would kill Cartwright if he made any such accusation to the authorities.

After Cartwright returned to Macon County, Sanders continued to make treats against him. The last known threat Sanders made against Cartwright was on October 12, 1880, the day before the murder on the Square.

The autumn weather was nice in Lafayette, Tennessee on October 13, 1880. At least it was nice enough that Wednesday for young men to congregate to the town square and sit outside in front of Johnson's Inn. Several young men including Cartwright and Sanders gathered in front of the hotel on that day. They engaged in idle conversation and there was some laughter, but there wasn't any rowdiness or arguments, just "playful" banter.

Cartwright, as was usual for him, was drinking quite heavily. What was unusual was that he had a gun in his possession. Contrary to the stereotype, Tennesseans of those days did not usually walk around with loaded pistols strapped to their hips. Many had pistols for home protection and most households had shotguns and rifles for hunting game, but it was rare to see anyone walking around town with a firearm.

Neither Sanders, nor any of the other men were armed, yet Cartwright did not seem threatening to them. In fact, they decided to have a little fun with the intoxicated young man. One of the men said to Joe Cartwright, "Does carrying a gun make you drunk? If it does, I'll get me one."

Then Sanders chimed in, "If it makes you drunk, then pass it around and we will all have a spree."

Cartwright didn't seem to mind the others having a little gentle fun at his expense and the conversation moved on to other things. A few minutes later, the group broke up with Cartwright and Sanders going in opposite directions. There was no sign of trouble between the two.

Between one and two hours later, Sanders and two other men returned to the front of the Johnson's Inn. The owner of the hotel joined them. All four men sat and passed the time in idle chitchat. The conversation was jovial, but not loud.

A few minutes after the conversation began, the hotel owner saw Cartwright approaching them. Joe was still carrying his gun. Someone turned to Sanders and asked him if he wasn't "uneasy" at the thought that Cartwright might attack him.

Sanders replied, "No, we have been at odds, but we have agreed to drop it, and we speak when we pass."

Joe Cartwright continued to walk slowly and deliberately toward the men in front of the hotel. When he was near them, he stepped into the street to make his way around those between him and Sanders. Then he stepped directly in front of, and very close to, his intended victim.

Evidently, Sanders still didn't sense any danger, because he remained seated when Cartwright stepped in front of him. The lack of immediate reaction on the part of Sanders proved to be a fatal mistake.

Suddenly, in a loud, shaking voice slurred by alcohol, an enraged Cartwright yelled at Sanders "Goddamn you! I suppose you have something against me!"

Before the unarmed Sanders could retort, Cartwright raised his pistol, pointed it, and pulled the trigger. The pistol's report shook the windows of the buildings on that side of Lafayette's Public Square.

Cartwright was so near Sanders that despite his intoxication, he could not miss his target. The bullet ripped through Sanders' body, leaving him mortally wounded.

Cartwright had evidently not given any previous thought to getting away. He walked a short distance away from the Public Square, but when he looked back and realized that some townsfolk were pursuing him, he took flight across an open field.

Despite his frantic attempt to exit the scene, subduing Cartwright was easy. His captors hauled him back and turned him over to newly elected Macon County Sheriff W. T. Gray. Gray housed the young man in jail until the District Attorney preferred charges.

Hugh Sanders died within hours of the shooting and after reviewing the facts, the

District Attorney charged Cartwright with first-degree murder.

The First Murder Trial

Cartwright went on trial in the Circuit Court at Lafayette with Judge N. W. McConnell of Hartsville presiding over the proceedings.

Since there was no question as to the facts in the case, the only matter for adjudication was one of justification. The prosecutor for the state of Tennessee saw no mitigating circumstances. He charged that Joe Cartwright was guilty of premeditated murder. The prosecutor asked for the court to sentence Cartwright to death.

Cartwright entered a plea of not guilty claiming his drunkenness made him unable to act rationally.

Cartwright's attorneys touted the fact that he came from a good family. Joe's father was Enoch "E. G." E. G. was a postmaster and he served for more than two decades as Macon County Register of Deeds. Few men in Macon County were as respected as E. G. Cartwright was.

Joe's family stood by him at his murder trial. His father, mother (Sarah W. *Smithwick* Cartwright), and older sister (Nancy) all testified in his defense. They all agreed that Cartwright had been drinking heavily for at least three years. However, considering his degree of addiction, it is likely that he had been a drunkard for much longer than that.

Cartwright's family members also testified that that had witnessed Joe experience *DTs* (*delirium tremens*). *DT*s is the name given to the withdrawals those addicted to alcohol sometimes experience when deprived of booze for a period. Of course, Cartwright could not have been suffering from *DT*s on the day of the killings, because he was drinking. However, it is likely that few in the courtroom understood alcohol withdrawal. Cartwright's family members also offered that Joe was "not of sound mind."

Cartwright's father told the court that Joe was "wild and very drunk" on the day of the homicide. He said Joe was out of his mind and worse that day than he had been for months. If that was true, Joe became "wild" after his first encounter with Sanders that day. He certainly wasn't out of his mind beforehand.

The elder Cartwright had more to offer as well. He said he was attending his duties at the post office on that fateful Wednesday and soon after Hugh Sanders left the group in front of Johnson's Inn, he came into the post office and asked for a letter.

The postmaster said Sanders behaved strangely while he was in the post office. He continued that Sanders kept his hands in his pockets the whole time, looked around nervously, and then walked quickly out of the building.

The elder Cartwright continued that a few moments after Sanders departed, Joe entered the post office. The elder Cartwright told his son about his strange encounter with Sanders. He said he didn't like the way Sanders acted and he feared that Joe's enemy was up to no good. E. G. advised his son to go home before Sanders could work any mischief.

Joe promised his father that he would go home, but only after he talked to a local merchant named Willie Claiborne. After he left the post office – and only a few minuets before he killed Sanders – Joe walked past Claiborne's store and peered inside, apparently trying without success to locate the owner.

Sarah Cartwright testified that the previous accusations against Joe left her son depressed. She continued, "Charging him with stealing the wine had put him below the respect of decent people." Perhaps Sarah Cartwright didn't realize that her son's continuous displays of public intoxication had caused "decent people" to lose respect for him long before the church had its wine pilfered.

State witnesses countered Cartwright's family by testifying that Joe was perfectly sane at the time of the slaying and that, in fact, he was always of sound mind.

All witnesses agreed that Cartwright was drinking on the day of the murder. However, testimony differed as to the extent of his drunkenness. Those testifying in his defense stated that he was very drunk, those testifying against him contended that he was "drinking, but was not drunk." Yet, even those testifying against him conceded that Cartwright was under the influence of alcohol to some degree.

After the testimony, the judge McConnell charged the jury on the subject of drunkenness as follows:

"Voluntary drunkenness is no excuse for the commission of a crime, but it may be looked to, to ascertain whether the offense has been committed or not. We have seen to commit murder in the first-degree the killing must be done willfully, deliberately, premeditatedly, and with malice aforethought. This requires certain states of the mind, and the question of the intoxication of the prisoner may be looked to, to see whether at the time of the killing he had these states of mind. Was he so intoxicated that he was incapable of giving the consent of his will to the killing, or of deliberating and premeditating the deed; if he was, then he cannot be guilty of murder in the first-degree. But if he was capable of willing, deliberating and premeditating the deed, then he is capable of committing murder in the first-degree, notwithstanding his intoxication, and it can be no excuse for him. The only effect that voluntary drunkenness can have in any event, is to reduce the crime from murder in the first to murder in the second-degree. It is never ground of entire justification, except it amounts to insanity, as will hereafter be explained to you."

McConnell continued with his charge. "If you believe, beyond a reasonable doubt, he (Cartwright) shot Sanders in malice, not intending to kill him but did do it, or if you find he was so intoxicated that he was not capable of that deliberation or premeditation necessary to make murder in the first-degree, or you have a reasonable doubt how this is, you should find him guilty of murder in the second-degree."

The jury, based on the evidence, the testimony, and the judge's charge, found Joe Cartwright guilty of first-degree murder and ordered him to suffer death by hanging.

Cartwright's attorneys I. L. Roark and John G. Guild filed an immediate appeal with the Tennessee Supreme Court claiming that Judge McConnell charged the jury in error. The Supreme Court heard the appeal in December 1881.

After hearing the arguments, the Supreme Court chose to render its decision based completely on a purely technical interpretation of previous court rulings regarding homicides committed by drunken men. The Court did not consider the evidence in regard to the Sanders killing.

The justices ruled that judge McConnell's charge to the jury was in error because he made the "whole effect" of Cartwright's "intoxication in reducing the killing to murder in the second-degree depend upon whether the drunkenness was to such an extent as to render the prisoner incapable of deliberation and premeditation.

The High Court continued "A degree of intoxication short of this may, when taken in connection with the other facts, show that the killing resulted from a purpose formed in passion, and not deliberately and premeditatedly; and although there be no adequate provocation to reduce the offense to manslaughter, yet if in this mode the want of deliberation and premeditation appear, it may be reduced to murder in the second-degree.

"In a case involving life, we do not feel ourselves at liberty to overlook this error, whatever we might think of the facts. The prisoner is entitled to a correct exposition of the law.

"The judgment must, therefore, be reversed and the cause remanded for a new trial."

The Second Murder Trial

Cartwright did not hang for killing Hugh Sanders, but neither did he get away with the murder. The state prosecutor was determined to convict Cartwright and he filed charges again.

Wanting to give their client the best opportunity at an acquittal, Cartwright's lawyers requested a change in venue and the second trial took place in nearby Hartsville, Tennessee. As he did in the first trial, Judge McConnell presided.

A new jury heard the evidence, and this jury convicted Joe Cartwright of second-degree murder. This time he received a sentence of 15 years in prison.

Naturally, Cartwright's attorneys this time around, J. J. Turner, I. L. Roark, and the McMurry & Hamilton law firm, did not let the verdict go unchallenged. They appealed and the case wound its way back to the Tennessee Supreme Court.

Cartwright's lawyers alleged before the High Court that Judge McConnell had made nine errors during the trial, any one of which, if sustained, amounted to grounds for reversal.

The most serious of the alleged errors centered on the statement of defense witness Arnez Diaz.

The Diaz testimony was that Hugh Sanders feared that Cartwright would accuse him of stealing the wine from the Church of Christ. According to Diaz, Sanders loaded a gun and said he would kill Cartwright if he made such an accusation.

Diaz could not attend the trial, but the defense attorneys believed the court would allow them to read Diaz's deposition to the jury. However, when the defense attempted to read Diaz's statement, the prosecution objected and the judge barred the testimony.

The Supreme Court ruled that the judge was within his authority to sustain the prosecutor's objection to a statement by a witness that could not be cross-examined. Beyond that, the Justices ruled that since Cartwright never learned of the alleged threat by Sanders, the Diaz testimony proved nothing and it had no bearing on the case.

Cartwright's legal team also claimed that jury members discussed the case with outsiders while sequestered at Hartsville's Allen Hotel. Cartwright's attorneys could not provide proof of the allegation. Without any evidence to prove the defense claim, the Supreme Court rejected it.

Likewise, the High Court reviewed and rejected the other seven claims of error made by the defense and they allowed the verdict to stand.

Chief Justice James W. Deaderick wrote the Supreme Court's decision. Deaderick was no fan of Joe Cartwright. At the end of the ruling Deaderick slammed Joe Cartwright with a scathing rebuke:

"The defendant deliberately loaded his gun with slugs, sought the deceased, and found him sitting in front of the hotel in conversation with others, utterly unsuspicious of danger, when defendant stepped within a few feet of him, and shot him."

The Davidson County Sheriff delivered Cartwright to the Tennessee State Penitentiary on March 5, 1884.

The Murder of Joe Cartwright

As is the case with most alcoholics, Joe Cartwright never went into recovery. Despite the pain and suffering alcohol had caused him and his family, he continued to drink heavily for the balance of his life.

Even on the evening of his death, Cartwright consumed several alcoholic beverages. Of course, when he bellied up to the bar on Tuesday, September 3, 1895, he had no idea that he would never see his wife or his four children again.

After drinking for several hours, Cartwright was certainly drunk. He departed on foot for sometime after 7 o'clock that evening. At about 8 o'clock Cartwright's drinking buddies heard two shots ring out from the direction Cartwright was walking, but no one cared enough about him to investigate.

The next morning, a local citizen found the bloodstained corpse of Joe Cartwright in the road just outside of Lafayette. There was no doubt that foul play was involved.

The coroner determined that Joe Cartwright suffered two gunshot wounds to the head. One lead ball entered his nose and exited the back of his head near the base of his skull. The second bullet entered his head above his right ear and traveled downward. The murderer fired at least one of the rounds from very close range causing powder burns on Cartwright's face.

Macon County Sheriff James W. King surveyed the scene and surmised that the shots the other drinkers heard on the evening of September 3 were the ones that killed Joe Cartwright. However, he could not be certain his assumption was correct.

Sheriff King had no eyewitnesses, or other evidence implicating anyone in the shooting. The investigation went nowhere and Joe Cartwright's murderer or murderers escaped justice.

Sources.

"A Cold Blooded Murder at Lafayette." *The Daily American* October 15, 1880, page 1.

Blankenship, Harold G. *History of Macon County, Tennessee.* Tompkinsville, Kentucky: Monroe County Press, 1986, pages 29, 139, 155.

"Brought Here from Lafayette." *The Daily American*, January 9, 1882, page 4.

"Candidates for Stripes." *The Daily American*, March 3, 1884, page 4.

"County Jail Notes." *The Daily American*, February 5, 1884, page 5.

Courier Journal, (Louisville, Kentucky), September 6, 1895, page 1.

"His Second Appeal: The Case of a Convicted Murderer Twice Before the Supreme Court." *The Daily American*, February 6, 1884, page 4.

"Jail Jottings." *The Daily American*, January 12, 1881, page 1.

Lea, Benjamin, Attorney General and Reporter. "Cartwright v. The State" in *Reports of Cases Argued and Determined in the Supreme Court of Tennessee, for the Eastern Division, December Term, 1881, for the Middle Division, December Term, 1881, and for the Western Division, April Term 1882, Volume VIII*. Nashville: Travel Law Book Publisher, 1882, pages 376-386.

Lea, Benjamin, Attorney General and Reporter. "Cartwright v. The State" in *Reports of Cases Argued and Determined in the Supreme Court of Tennessee, for the Eastern Division, September Term, 1883, for the Middle Division, December Term, 1883, and for the Western Division, April Term 1882, Volume VIII*. Nashville: Travel Law Book Publisher, 1884, pages 620-630.

"Mysterious Killing: Dead Body of Joe Cartwright Found in the Road near Lafayette." *The Nashville American*, September 6, 1895, page 1.

"Placed in Jail for Safe Keeping." *The Daily American*, September 2, 1881, page 4.

"Sent to Pen." *The Daily American*, March 6, 1884, page 5.

2. Wildcatters Shoot Deputy

OVER the years, moonshiners in Macon County produced and sold millions of gallons of illicit liquor. Long before the enactment of National Prohibition, The Internal Revenue Service took interest in these illegal moonshine operations.

The "wildcatters," as they were called, didn't pay taxes on their sales and the IRS strove to shut them down. To accomplish this, the IRS deputized agents and tasked them to scour the rough country of Macon County in search of wildcatters. Once they located illicit moonshine operations, the agents dumped the illegal liquor, destroyed the stills and other whiskey making equipment, and arrested any of the moonshiners they could capture.

The job of a revenue agent was a dangerous one. On March 18, 1881, United States Deputy Marshals Henry Seagraves and J. M. Phillips rode their horses from Lafayette in the direction of Red Boiling Springs. They had heard rumors of a large wildcat distillery in the area and they meandered through the deep woods looking for it.

After several hours of fruitless investigation, the two men decided to break off the search and return to Lafayette. As they headed through the deep undergrowth toward the main road that would lead them back to town, Phillips rode down a steep grade into one hollow and Seagraves rode into another one.

Although separated by only about 200 yards, the Deputies lost sight of each other.

Suddenly, two moonshiners, both on foot and armed with rifles, confronted Phillips. In ominous tones, the men ordered Phillips to turn around and go back. Before Phillips could react, one of the men raised and fired his rifle. The lead ball struck Phillips in the upper arm and lodged in the bone. As Phillips began to dismount, the murderous moonshiner grabbed his partner's rifle and fired *it* at Phillips, this time missing the Revenuer. Deputy Phillips finished dismounting, drew his pistol, but he did not fire it. Instead, he rushed forward, and using it like a hammer, struck the moonshiner on the head with the pistol stock twice.

Seagraves heard the gunfire and he rode as quickly as he could toward the combatants. Seeing Seagraves, the moonshiners ran to their distillery that was only 50 or 60 yards away. The wildcatters tried to hide behind their still house as the deputies rode up. When the agents were about 40 yards from the still house, one of the moonshiners took a shot at Seagraves, but missed.

An unseen ally of the moonshiners yelled out from inside the still house, "You had better get away from there or they will kill you!"

With that, the two moonshiners ran about 60 yards away from the back of the still house and took up positions behind a stack of logs. Phillips fired once at the men as they hunkered behind the logs, but he did not hit anyone.

Feeling they did not have the weaponry to outgun the outlaws, and with the bleeding Phillips being in need of medical attention, the raiders broke off the firefight and returned to Lafayette without accomplishing anything.

Phillips was a fortunate man. His wound was quite painful, but it was not life threatening. Upon returning to Lafayette, he visited Dr. Marlin Luther Kirby for treatment. Dr. Kirby tried to extract the bullet embedded the Deputy's humerus bone. But after several attempts at digging it out, the doctor gave up and let the slug remain where it was.

Sources.

Blankenship, Harold G. *History of Macon County, Tennessee.* Tompkinsville, Kentucky: Monroe County Press, 1986, page 137.

Gammon, CL. *Revenue Raiders: Macon County's Whiskey War.* Lafayette, Tennessee: Deep Read Press, 2022, pages 46-48.

"Raiding the Wild Cats." *The Daily American*, March 22, 1881, page 4.

3. Deputy Murdered

LESS than three weeks after the shootout described in the previous chapter, Deputy US Marshal Henry Seagraves lost his life in the line of duty.

Seagraves was about 50 and he was a man of fierce courage. He had worked in the service of the federal government for about two years. He was also a family man. He had a wife and three children.

The first news of the Seagraves murder came from a man named John Wallace. Wallace was a sawmill operator living at the edge of Macon County near the Sumner County line. He related that Seagraves intended to spend the night of April 8, 1881 at a friend's house before returning to Lafayette the next morning. Wallace continued that five men called Seagraves out, forced him into the woods, and then shot him twice in the head.

The original story proved inaccurate, but the true story was just as disturbing. On the morning of April 7, Seagraves and an agent named Cox went to Sumner County intent on making several arrests. They spent that entire day and much of the next in Sumner County, before heading toward home.

After nightfall on April 8, the two stopped about 12 miles west of Lafayette near the Siloam Church at the home of a man named

Rutherford. Beyond resting a bit, the men had dinner while their horses fed.

After dining, in a hurry to get started home, Seagraves went outside to saddle the horses and Rutherford joined him. While the men worked with the horses, they heard pistol shots coming from the direction of a cabin belonging to African American man.

Surprised, Seagraves asked, "What does that mean?"

Rutherford responded, "I don't know; the colored man has nothing to shoot with."

More curious than concerned, Seagraves told Rutherford, "Put out your lantern and I will go see what it is?"

Seagraves started in the direction of the cabin, which was about 100 yards away. When he was near, he called out asking if anything was wrong.

A voice coming from inside the cabin answered, "Who is there?"

As he continued forward, Deputy Seagraves answered with his name and his title.

The officer never made it to the cabin. A shot rang out and Seagraves, hit in the chest by the bullet, died instantly.

After killing Seagraves, the murderers, who previously forced themselves into the cabin, ordered the owner to take a light and go see what was outside. The intimidated man resisted for a few minutes, but he complied eventually. He had not gone far when he came across the lifeless body of Deputy Seagraves. The frightened man hurriedly returned to the cabin and told the criminals what he had seen.

The murderers ordered the man to go back outside and to drag the corpse inside the cabin. This time the man mustered a remarkable amount of courage and refused to go back to the body, even upon threats of death. Frustrated, the criminals bound the cabin owner, took a lantern, and went outside themselves.

The murderers searched Seagraves, took his pistol, pocket watch, and whatever money he had on his person. Perhaps in an attempt to convince anyone listening that they were Native Americans, the murderers "whooped and hollered" like wild men as they took the dead man's possessions. They did not drag him to the cabin. Instead, they left Seagraves where he fell.

Later, when the authorities untied the man he told them that four armed men came to his home before the killing and asked if Seagraves and Cox were at the Rutherford place. Then, they forced him to go over to Rutherford's property to find out. While there, he observed the horses, and reported to the criminals that Seagraves was indeed at Rutherford's home. The criminals evidently fired the shot to lure Seagraves to them.

There was no doubt that the killers knew Seagraves. At first, the United States Marshal's office surmised that the motive for the murder was robbery. The Marshal's office reasoned that the killers thought Seagraves probably had a large sum of money he had collected performance of his duty in Sumner County.

Almost two weeks after the Seagraves murder the Internal Revenue Service, issued its official opinion. The IRS contradicted the US Marshal's office by stating that angry Sumner County moonshiners killed Seagraves in retaliation for his breaking up their operations.

There is a third version of this strange story. In this version, Seagraves came upon a still and a moonshiner named John Bradley murdered him. The inscription on the tombstone of Henry Seagraves reads, "A revenue officer shot by John Bradley at a still."

Sources.

Gammon, CL. *Revenue Raiders: Macon County's Whiskey War*. Lafayette, Tennessee: Deep Read Press, 2022, pages 48-51.

"Reported Outrage." *The Daily American*, April 10 1881, page 1.

"Seagraves Murder." *The Daily American*, April 12, 1881, page 4.

"The Murder of Seagraves." *The Daily American*, April 20, 1881, page 1.

4. Deputy Marshal Wounded

DEPUTY United States Marshal J. M. Phillips was an impressive figure. He was about 40, stood a little above average in height, was very strong, muscular, and lean. He had light blue eyes, a lantern jaw, and a few sprigs of gray whiskers had sprouted in his beard.

Phillips was an old school swashbuckler, a fearless and determined deputy, a man willing to spend days in hostile country, to endure harsh weather, and to face even the most desperate moonshiner. In short, he had the perfect personality for a Revenuer.

Phillips was also lucky – incredibly lucky. The injury he received in the gun battle related in Chapter 2 was minor compared to other wounds he received. Once, a moonshiner shot him in the chest with the bullet just missing his heart and exiting his back without contacting any major organ.

On March 18, 1882, Phillips barely escaped death again. Phillips was in the deep woods of Macon County searching for two specific moonshiners. It was about dusk as he rode slowly through the tall vegetation near a house he believed the moonshiners occupied.

Suddenly, the moonshiners stepped out into the open mere feet from Phillips. The surprised Deputy stopped his horse and tried to draw his revolver as quickly as possible. He was not quick enough. One of the moonshiners raised his rifle and fired. The molten lead ball struck Phillips in the right wrist shattering the bone.

The second moonshiner raised his rifle, but Phillips spurred his horse and when it bolted forward, the moonshiner lost his aim. Phillips took the opportunity to return fire, but being aboard the startled horse and with his wrist bone splintered, it is little wonder that the Deputy's shot went astray.

Unable to reload their weapons without risking Phillips shooting them both dead, the moonshiners turned and spirited into the thick, quickly darkening woods. Phillips emptied his pistol into the shadows at the receding outlaws, but he hit neither of them.

Despite his wound, Phillips still had a job to do. He dismounted, reloaded, and continued his search for the distillery. Within 30 minutes, he had found and destroyed the still, but he never caught up with the moonshiners who had attempted to murder him.

Sources.

Gammon, CL. *Revenue Raiders: Macon County's Whiskey War*. Lafayette, Tennessee: Deep Read Press, 2022, pages 52-53.

"Life at Stake." *The Daily American*, October 26, 1885, page 1.

5. Murder at Eulia Church

IN previous times, churches were more than mere places of worship; they were centers of rural communities. Some people attended church for social interaction as much as for anything else. Sadly, churches were sometimes the scenes of fights and even murders.

On Sunday evening, October 17, 1886, 23-year-old Miller Gammon and a man identified as "Saylors" were at the little country church in the Eulia community. Gammon and Saylor engaged in an argument over a woman. The disagreement soon turned violent and deadly.

Gammon suddenly drew his knife and slashed Saylors across the hand and both cheeks. Then, Gammon struck another blow with his knife blade disemboweling Saylors. The victim died on the spot.

Gammon ran away from the scene. Authorities in Coatstown (now called Westmoreland) telephoned Gallatin and requested that Marshal J. C. Clark be on the outlook for the desperate fugitive and Clark began a manhunt for Gammon.

Sources.

Cothron, Judy M. (editor). *Macon County, Tennessee: 1870 & 1880 Census*, (1880 Section). Lafayette, Tennessee: Macon County Historical Society, 1995, page 33.

"Fugitive from Justice." *The Daily American,* October 19, 1886, page 5.

6. Fracas at a Circus

A series of a few unrelated and isolated events caused Macon County residents to get a reputation for troublemaking and general rowdiness. There are numerous accounts, many of them false, of hooligans from Macon County traveling to nearby towns and starting brawls for no good reason. The underserved reputation for the anti-social behavior and general misconduct of Macon County citizens lingered for decades.

The Tennessee counties of Macon and Trousdale adjoin each other and less than twenty miles separate their respective county seats (Lafayette and Hartsville). For about the past 150 years the residents of the two counties have engaged in a, mostly, friendly rivalry. Yet, occasionally, the rivalry has turned violent. At least, there have been reports of violence among citizens of the two counties.

On the afternoon of May 30, 1887, a huge crowd of between 1,500 and 5,000 came to Hartsville from across middle Tennessee and southern Kentucky. To give an idea of the size of the crowd, the population of Hartsville in those days was fewer than 1,000. The visitors squeezed into Hartsville to see a traveling show variously called "George DeHaven's Show" and "DeHaven's Imperial Circus."

A large group shoved their way into the Big Top tent to see the first show of the day, and trouble soon began.

First, a massive torrent of rain poured down threatening to conclude the festivities before they hardly got underway. However, organizers decided that "the show must go on" and they continued with the performance.

Then, a more serious incident occurred. According to reports, just as the show began, between 25 and 30 "roughs" from Macon County began "fighting, cursing, and drinking." The ruffians formed a circle in the center of the tent and passed around bottles of rotgut whiskey among themselves.

The situation became even uglier when the thugs brandished "knives, sticks, and pistols" and lashed out at other audience members with them. No one received serious injuries, but some audience members received cuts and bruises. The dozen or so Trousdale County deputies on the scene attempted to control the angry mob of hooligans, but outnumbered and overmatched, they failed restore order.

The melee threatened to grow into a general riot, and show organizers had little recourse but to suspend the show. They cancelled the program scheduled for that night as well.

Sources.

"Fight in a Circus." *The Daily American*, June 1, 1887, page 1.

Slout, William L., editor. *Olympians of the Sawdust Circle: A Biographical Dictionary of the Nineteenth Century American Circus*. San Bernardino California: Borgo Press, 2010.

7. A Child Abduction

AMBER Alerts signifying child abductions are an all too common occurrences in today's world. Yet, child abductions, especially by disgruntled parents, have been with us since the dawn of time.

Elisha White lived in Montgomery County, Tennessee with his wife and their 2-year-old son. The couple did not get along well with each other. Eventually, Elisha left his spouse and child in Montgomery County and moved to Macon County.

Abandoned, Mrs. White filed for divorce. Before the court finalized the divorce, Elisha White returned to Montgomery County with three compatriots. Once there, they disguised themselves and broke into Mrs. White's home. The only other adult in the home was Mrs. White's mother. The two women could not resist the four men and White and his associates kidnapped the little boy forcibly and took him back to Macon County with them.

Despite her husband's disguise, Mrs. White recognized him and reported the kidnapping. The Montgomery County Sheriff procured a warrant and went to Macon County in search of Elisha White and the little boy. Finding the kidnapper proved rather easy and the Sheriff arrested White, brought him back to Clarksville, and lodged him in the Montgomery County jail.

The toddler was uninjured and the Sheriff reunited the mother and her child.

Source.

"Clarksville: Arrested for Kidnapping." *The Daily American*, August 30, 1887, page 1.

8. Disrupted Church Services

INTERRUPTING religious meetings was not a common occurrence in the late 19th Century, but it did happen. Authorities took such disruptions seriously and looked upon them dimly.

On September 9, 1888, about 8 miles from Carthage, in the Smith County community of Riddleton, three "roughs" from Macon County had a "difficulty" outside a church and succeeded in breaking up the services. Authorities identified the ruffians as Lambert Cothron, Bud Burrow, and a person named Woodmore. Woodmore had a pistol and while the other two were unarmed, they pretended to have guns.

Constables, assisted by Smith County residents, arrested Burrow and Cothron and they stood trial before a Justice of the Peace. The Justice ordered Burrow to pay a fine of $50 and court costs. Burrow said he could not pay the full amount. He requested a reduction of the fine to $25 and the Justice agreed. Cothron paid a $4 fine and costs. Woodmore remained at large.

Most Smith County residents disapproved of the slap on the wrist the ruffians from Macon County received. They felt Burrow and Cothron deserved much harsher punishment, including jail time.

The verdict evidently didn't teach Cothron any kind of a lesson. Before going home, he rode his horse up and down the road near the church, cursed at the parishioners, and promised to bring back a large gang from Macon County to disrupt the church services again. Thankfully, he never made good his threat.

Sources.

Cothron, Judy M. (editor). *Macon County, Tennessee: 1870 & 1880 Census*, Lafayette, Tennessee: Macon County Historical Society, 1995, (1880 Section) page 74.

"Smith County: Ruffians Break up a Religious Gathering – Pleading for Mercy before the Law." *The Daily American*, September 14, 1888, page 7.

9. Shootout Kills Horse

UNTIL recently, most citizens of Macon County were farmers. In the 19th Century, the success of most farms depended upon the quality of the beasts of burden farmers had at their disposal. Thus, losing a good animal could spell disaster for a farm family.

During the evening of the November 10, 1888, Sam Parker and a man named Robertson had a dispute at the Ebenezer Church in southern Macon County. The argument escalated into gunplay and the two men began shooting at each other.

Neither man suffered any wound, but there was an unintended victim. One of the stray bullets caused collateral damage when it struck and killed a "fine mare" belonging to Billy Cothron. The death of the animal represented a major financial loss to the horse's owner.

Authorities arrested and jailed Robertson. They scheduled his trial for later in that November.

Source.

"Shooting in Macon County." *The Daily American*, November 15, 1888, page 3.

10. A Mail Robbery

THERE was a time when citizens routinely sent large sums of cash by way of the United States mail. This made mail carriers ready targets of highwaymen looking to turn a fast and easy buck. Additionally, the massive river of dollars flowing through the mails sometimes tempted unscrupulous postal workers to take some of the cash for themselves.

Near the end of February 1889, a postal carrier named Elijah Snyder reported to Red Boiling Springs Postmaster H. J. Cloyd that he had been the victim of a robbery. Snyder, who was only 18-years-old, related that as he was going along his route (19484 from Celina, Tennessee) four masked men accosted him on the road about one mile east of Red Boiling Springs. He said the armed men took his mail pouch from him and rode away with it.

Cloyd was skeptical of Snyder's story and he searched the young mail carrier. Although he didn't find anything incriminating on Snyder, Cloyd remained unconvinced that the young man was telling the truth.

With nothing else to go on, Cloyd exercised the police powers accorded him as a United States postmaster. He formed a posse and rode to the location where Snyder swore the four men robbed him. After a short search, Cloyd and his deputies found Snyder's discarded mailbag about 30 or 40 yards off the roadway. Someone had slit open the bag and had taken the contents of three registered letters, leaving the envelopes behind. A letter bound for Nashville originated in Celina. Another one addressed to a location in Nashville originated in Kentucky. The third came from Butler's Landing (near Celina) and was on its way to New Haven, Connecticut.

Finding physical evidence of the crime only strengthened Cloyd's suspicion of Snyder. He placed the youthful mail carrier under strong questioning and Snyder eventually broke down. Snyder admitted there were no masked bandits. He then confessed to the robbery. After he confessed, Snyder told Cloyd where he had hidden the money and the postmaster retrieved it.

Macon County Sheriff W. L. Tuck packed Snyder safely away in jail and Cloyd wrote to the United States District Attorney General in Nashville informing the prosecutor of the situation.

On April 22, 1889, Snyder stood trial in the United States District Court and entered a guilty plea. The judge fined Snyder $100, but since the mail thief was underage, the judge did not order Snyder to an adult prison. Instead, Snyder received a sentence of one year's confinement in the Federal Reformatory for Boys at Elmira, New York.

Sources.

"A Year at Elmira." *The Daily American*, April 23, 1880, page 4.

Blankenship, Harold G. *History of Macon County, Tennessee.* Tompkinsville, Kentucky: Monroe County Press, 1986, page 155.

Cothron, Judy M. (editor). *Macon County, Tennessee: 1870 & 1880 Census,* (1880 Section). Lafayette, Tennessee: Macon County Historical Society, 1995, pages 12, 67.

"He Lost all of His Nerve." *The Daily American,* March 5, 1880, page 4.

11. Rapist on the Loose

EPPERSON Springs was home to a major resort in the western section of Macon County in the 19th and early 20th centuries. Every summer, vacationers from across the United States traveled to Epperson Springs for relaxation and the health benefits of mineral waters offered there. Visitors often took the train to nearby Westmoreland and then rode a horse-drawn taxi, called a "hack," the short distance to the resort.

In the middle of July 1888, a young woman from Nashville named Alice Parkerson got off the train in Westmoreland. Traveling alone, she wasn't headed for the resort at Epperson Springs. Her destination was the home of relatives in the Eulia community.

The hack driver at the train station that day was a married father named Bud Gross. Gross told Parkerson that he would gladly take her where she wanted to go, but that he would have to drop the vacationers off at the resort first. She agreed.

Parkerson and several others boarded the hack late that afternoon and Gross began the short trip to Epperson Springs. All the passengers except Parkerson got off the hack at the resort. It was past dark when Gross and Parkerson departed Epperson Springs for the final leg of the woman's journey.

The heavily wooded area between Epperson Springs and the young woman's destination was sparsely populated and no one would likely notice a hack hidden among the trees off the side of the road. According to Parkerson, Gross pulled the hack off the roadway and after she rejected his sexual advances, he raped her forcibly. Parkerson continued that after the attack, Gross took her to the home of her relatives, put her out, and drove away.

Her ordeal traumatized Alice and she couldn't bring herself to report the incident for about three weeks. When Alice made the allegation, the authorities issued a warrant for the arrest of Gross and took him into custody without incident.

Gross appeared before Justice of the Peace W. M. Durham on August 2, . Durham set bond for Gross at $1,000 and bound him over for trial at the next session of the Circuit Court in Lafayette. Gross said he didn't have $1,000 in cash. He asked the Justice to allow him to go to Westmoreland and secure the services of a bail bondsman. Durham agreed and he ordered Constable Joseph R. "Joe" Weatherford to transport Gross to Westmoreland to meet with the bondsman.

Constable Weatherford was of the advanced age of 66, and Gross was able to get away from him easily and go on the lamb. Naturally, a manhunt followed.

Source.

"A Dastardly Deed." *The Daily American*, August 4, 1889, page 1.

12. Court Charges Forty-Seven

MANY local officials in Tennessee carried the nickname "whiskey men." The whiskey men didn't care if citizens added to their meager farm incomes by churning out and selling moonshine whiskey. Because of the apathy and lax enforcement of liquor laws by whiskey men, interdiction of outlaw drink alcohol declined for several years.

The newly inaugurated President, Benjamin Harrison was strongly anti-liquor. Thus, it is not surprising that in 1889, Federal efforts to stamp out wildcatters in Macon and other counties in the "Upper Country" increased dramatically.

At the October 1889 session of Federal Court, 47 citizens of Macon County stood accused of various crimes associated with moonshine operations. This was an amazing number when one considers that Macon County's population was fewer than 11,000. While more than one of every two hundred and fifty Macon County citizens went to court for liquor violations in October 1889 most of those involved in the illicit liquor trade remained undetected. While the total is uncertain, the number involved in the moonshine business in Macon County was very large indeed.

Some observers worried that the crackdown on wildcat liquor operations would damage the Macon County economy. In 1889, moonshine whiskey sold from between $1.50 and $2 per gallon and the average still could produce about four and one-half gallons daily. Thus, the average still could generate the hefty sum of $6.75 to $9 in income each day, and more than $3,000 yearly. Just fifty stills could generate in excess of $135,000 per annum.

Sources.

Gammon, CL. *Revenue Raiders: Macon County's Whiskey War*. Lafayette, Tennessee: Deep Read Press, 2022, page 56.

"Moonshine Beams." *The Daily American*, October 27, 1889, page 7.

13. A Blackmail Plot

THERE have always been smooth operating predators lurking about with the intention of victimizing others. W. H. Wright was the victim of a very pretty predator.

Wright engaged in "improper relations" with a married woman in Macon County. After the affair ended, the woman then went to Wright and attempted to extort money from him. She said that unless Wright paid her to remain silent, she would inform her husband of the tawdry affair. Wright doubted the woman would reveal the relationship and he refused to submit to her demands.

The adulterer wasn't bluffing. Wright soon found himself facing charges in both civil and criminal court. The woman filed a civil suit requesting damages. Additionally, the District Attorney General charged Wright with criminal assault. Wright didn't want to go through the spectacle of a public trial. He agreed to a compromise in which he would pay $150 in exchange for having all charges against him dropped.

Wright paid the $150, but it didn't end his legal troubles. While the woman dropped the claim for damages, she refused to drop assault charge against Wright. The criminal case eventually went to trial and the jury acquitted him.

Exonerated by the jury, but not in the eyes of the public, Wright filed a petition requesting that Governor Robert Love Taylor pardon him. The trial judge and that Attorney General concurred that Wright deserved a full pardon.

After reviewing the Wright's request, on February 1, 1890, Taylor issued the pardon. Wright even had his $150 returned to him.

Source.

"Attempted Blackmail." *The Daily American* February 2, 1890, page 11.

14. Bullying Leads to Killing

BULLYING is a terrible thing. It can lead to violence or even death. Such was the case on Sunday, March 16, 1890.

It was about 3 o'clock that Sunday afternoon and Sidney (called "Elmore" by one reporter) Carver and his little brother were gathering firewood near their home in the Eulia community. Sidney was between 16 and 18 and he was protective of his sibling.

While Sidney was out of earshot, Thomas (called John in one report) Patterson came along and began bullying the younger Carver boy. Patterson, who was between 21 and 23, poked fun at the Carver child for being crossed-eyed.

The little Carver boy ran to Sidney and told him what Thomas Patterson had done. Sidney confronted Patterson immediately about the bullying, and Patterson denied doing anything to the boy. Unable to contain his anger, Sidney called Patterson a "damned liar," Patterson took offense and the two engaged in a fistfight.

Bigger and the stronger, Patterson had Sidney Carver overmatched. Patterson knocked Carver to the ground thrice, but Carver would not quit the fight. As Carver rose the third time, he drew his knife and stabbed Patterson under the arm. Then, Carver delivered the deathblow by ripping a terrible five-inch deep gash into Patterson's abdomen. Death overtook the mortally wounded Patterson about three hours later.

Justice of the Peace, W. M. Durham held an inquest and then issued an arrest warrant for Sidney Carver. However, Carver had already fled Macon County and authorities believed he was hiding somewhere in Kentucky.

Source.

"Slain on Sunday." *The Daily American*, March 19, 1890, page 2.

15. Wife Beater Slain

SPOUSAL abuse is a continuing blight on the world. During one Christmas holiday season, wife beating led to the death of the abuser.

John "Jack" Turner of the Salt Lick community sat in Macon County jail on December 24, 1890. He was serving a sentence for beating his wife, Louisa. That afternoon, Louisa came to the jail and begged the Sheriff to release her husband. The Sheriff agreed, let Turner out, and watched as the couple left for their home.

Sadly, the Turners did not enjoy a blissful holiday season. On the contrary, it turned into a nightmare for Louisa Turner. Immediately after they returned home, the ungrateful Jack Turner guzzled down several shots of liquor, and once he was drunk, he began to brutalize Louisa. Fearing for her life, Louisa got away from her demonic husband and ran to the house of a neighbor named Jenkins.

The day after Christmas, Turner, described as acting as if the Devil possessed him, showed up outside the Jenkins home. He threatened to kill everyone inside and he attempted to break down the front door of the Jenkins house. At that point, Jenkins grabbed his gun and shot Turner, killing him instantly.

The Sheriff brought Jenkins before a Justice of the Peace. The Justice determined that Jenkins had acted in defense of himself and Louisa Turner. That being the case, the Justice released Jenkins without binding him over for criminal trial.

Source.

"Possessed by Demon." *The Daily American*, January 14, 1891, page 6.

16. A Vicious Assault

ALL murders are senseless, but some murders are more brutal than others are. Such was the case of a murder of a Macon County man named Griffin.

During the summer of 1891, Griffin travelled to West Tennessee with a family by the name of Stovall. However, Griffin returned a few weeks later.

On November 15, 1891, witnesses saw Griffin in the company of two teenagers. The trio moved, apparently aimlessly, along Nashville Pike in Sumner County. At least one witness saw them together near Castalian Springs.

On November 16, a woman walked past the three who had secluded themselves behind a cedar thicket on the farm belonging to Humphrey Bate. The three were gambling and drinking whiskey, but they appeared peaceful enough.

When the woman returned later that day, she saw a battered and bloody Griffin lying prostrate and unconscious on the ground. She also saw playing cards strewn all around the badly injured man. The woman ran and got help. Those aiding Griffin carried him to a nearby church. Then, they telephoned doctors Woodson and Allen of Sumner County.

When the doctors arrived to treat Griffin, they found a grotesque figure. Someone had crushed Griffin's skull with something large and heavy, such as a wagon standard. Part of

Griffin's fractured skull was missing and a portion of his brain was exposed. It surprised the doctors that Griffin did not die immediately from his injuries. Their opinion was that the poor young man would expire without ever regaining consciousness.

It was common practice in those days for authorities to hire private detective services to investigate mysterious crimes. In this case, Sumner County officials contracted the Porter Detective Agency of Nashville to unravel the mystery of the assault on Griffin and to find the perpetrators.

Within days, the detective assigned to the case satisfied himself that he had identified the men that battered Griffin. The detective turned over his findings to the Sumner County Sheriff. Convinced, the Sheriff and a deputy went to Wilson County to arrest teenagers James Keel and Ernest McNichols. The two were staying at Hunter's Point on the Cumberland River.

The detective also informed members of the Nashville Police Department. Police officers from Nashville arrested Keel and McNichols before the Sumner County Sheriff and his deputy arrived. When the Sheriff finally got to Hunter's Point, the police officers turned the suspects over to him. The Sheriff transported the suspects to Gallatin, placed them in the county jail, and questioned them.

At first the teenagers (the youngest was fifteen and the other wasn't much older) refused to answer any questions. Later, they said that they were Wilson County farmers and that they never played cards with Griffin, or even met him for that matter. They also claimed to have alibis for the time of the assault.

The boys told plausible stories but the detective felt certain that his evidence proved them guilty. For one thing, the detective thought he could prove that Griffin and the accused boys had put a canoe in at Canoe Branch in Wilson County, had used it to cross the Cumberland River, and had then abandoned it. This evidence, if accurate, would prove that Keel and McNichols were lying about being with Griffin.

Meanwhile, Griffin did not die quickly. In fact, he displayed marked improvement. After a few days, Griffin regained consciousness and his helpers moved him back to his home in Macon County. There, another doctor took charge of the victim's treatment.

To the doctor's amazement, although Griffin couldn't speak or hear, he was able to get out of bed and walk around his room. The physician grew to believe that by some miracle, Griffin might live, regain his ability to speak, and at some point be able to identify those that tried to kill him.

The truth was that Griffin's injuries were too severe for him to survive very long and he soon passed without naming his attackers. With Griffin's death, the authorities charged Keel and McNichols with murder.

On December 12, 1891, Keel and McNichols went before two Justices of the Peace in Sumner County. The state prosecutors could not prove the accuracy of the story about the assailants taking the canoe across the Cumberland River with Griffin. Neither could they prove that the men seen with Griffin in the cedar thicket were Keel and McNichols. Finally, the prosecutors acknowledged that they lacked the evidence to mount a case against the two boys. With that, the Justices dismissed the case and sent Keel and McNichols on their way.

Sources.

"A Little Card Game." *The Daily American*, November 24, 1891, page 5.

"Griffin's Assailants." *The Daily American*, November 25, 1891, page 6.

"Keel and McNichols Dismissed." *The Daily American*, December 13, 1891, page 4.

17. Landlord Shot Down

RELATIONS between property owners and their tenants sometimes grow very strained. Too often, the bad relations escalate into violent altercations. One such altercation led to tragedy on the evening of July 17. 1892.

Henry Crook lived on a large farm owned by William Burrow in Macon County's Hillsdale community. Crook also worked as a laborer for Burrow. For some reason, Burrow instructed Crook to stay off a portion of the farm and Crook ignored him.

On a hot summer evening, Burrow caught Crook on the forbidden road and ordered Crook to turn around and to return the way he came. When Crook refused to go back, Burrow decided that he would force his tenant to obey instructions. The irate landowner picked up two rocks and he hurled one of them at Crook, but missed his target.

Before Burrow could launch his second projectile, Crook drew his single-shot cap and ball pistol and fired. The lead ball tore through Burrow's heart and he fell to the ground mortally wounded. Crook had no desire to face arrest and he fled the scene, leaving Burrow on the ground dead or dying.

Crook avoided arrest for more than a month and the frustrated authorities went so far as to offer a $50 reward his capture. Finally, on August 19, Sheriff Vance and Deputy James Flynn of Trousdale County located Crook in

Hartsville and took him into custody. They lodged him in the Trousdale County jail, but since the murder took place in Macon County, Crook's trial would have to take place there.

On March 20, 1893, Crook stood trial before Circuit Court Judge W. M. Hammock in the courthouse at Lafayette. The case was so notorious that as many gawking spectators as the courtroom could hold crowded inside to see the spectacle.

Crook had a strong defense team consisting of T. E. Foust, J.C. Marshall, J. E. Foust, and W. A. Smith. The District Attorney also had good assistance in I. L. Roark and W. C. Goad.

The jury convicted Crook of murder in the second-degree and sentenced him to ten years in the state penitentiary.

Sources.

Blankenship, Harold G. *History of Macon County, Tennessee.* Tompkinsville, Kentucky: Monroe County Press, 1986, page 139.

"Capture of Henry Crook." *The Daily American*, August 21, 1892, page 3.

"Murder of Nephew." *The Nashville American*, September 8, 1908, page 2.

"News Notes from Lafayette." *The Daily American*, March 29, 1893, page 6.

"Wm. Burrow Killed." *The Daily American*, July 19, 1892, page 1.

18. Fugitive Found

In the 1890s, much of Macon County was sparsely populated, heavily wooded, and in some ways still reminiscent of the rugged frontier of America's bygone days. Sometimes those trying to avoid justice attempted to take advantage of wild and woolly terrain of Macon County and use it as a hideout.

In February 1893, a man named Jack Marshall murdered Captain George Dixon in St. Mary Parish, Louisiana. Marshall escaped arrest and authorities there offered a $500 reward for his capture.

In late April 1893, a detective named John Anglea located a man in Macon County that fit the description of Jack Marshall perfectly. The detective arrested the suspect, transported him to Gallatin, and requested a court order to hold him until Anglea could obtain "proper evidence" from Louisiana.

The suspect claimed he was not Jack Marshall, but "Major Wise" and he said angrily "it would not do to call him that." Beyond his denial and threats, Marshall (or Wise) filed a writ of *habeas corpus* demanding that the authorities either charge with a crime or release him. A judge in Gallatin set a hearing for April 26 to settle the matter. He kept the suspect in jail in the meantime.

At the hearing, the judge rejected the writ of *habeas corpus* and ordered the man he believed to be Jack Marshall held until the state of Louisiana filed for the suspect's extradition back there to face charges for Captain Dixon's murder.

Sources.

"Charged With Murder." *The Daily American*, April 26, 1893, page 2

"At the Capitol." *The Daily American*, April 27, 1893, page 5.

19. A Horse Rustling Ring

BETWEEN 1,500,000 and 2,000,000 horses and mules died during the Civil War. This resulted in an equine shortage in America for decades afterwards. It is no wonder that in the Old West they hung horse thieves.

The horse and mule shortage affected life everywhere, especially in the southern United States. Even as late as the 1890s, good quality horses and mules were among a farmer's most important possessions. Considering the value of horses and mules, it is little wonder that in the 1890s rustling was in vogue across middle Tennessee, including Macon County.

In June 1893, authorities in Macon, Smith, Trousdale, and Sumner counties combined in an attempt to stamp out a ring of horse thieves operating in middle Tennessee. The law enforcement agents believed the rustlers were hiding in western Macon County, but they could not locate the secluded thieves. Despite all efforts to stop them, the rustlers continued to steal horses and mules almost at will.

On October 3, 1893, there were several more horses stolen near the border of Macon County and Allen County, Kentucky. The owners of the stolen horses included Susie Raynes, H. C. Cowan, and several others.

The authorities remained certain that the horse thieves were hiding the rustled animals in heavily wooded western of Macon County until they could transport them elsewhere and sell them. Detective John Anglea began an intensive search of the area. He soon arrested two brothers by the last name of Harrison near Westmoreland. Anglea accused the brothers of rustling a mule.

Suspicion grew that the Harrisons were part of the large ring of horse thieves. The suspicions were confirmed when searchers located rustled horses belonging to Frank Minnick and others. There was no doubt that the stealing was coordinated.

Anglea did not think arresting the Harrison brothers was anywhere near enough to end the rustling. The Harrisons were clearly not the leaders of the organized criminal operation. Anglea felt certain that the ring would continue to steal horses and mules until he and the other law enforcement agents broke it up and brought the criminal leaders to justice.

Despite all the best efforts of the authorities, horse thievery remained a problem in Macon County and the surrounding area for several years.

Sources.

Faust, Drew Gilpin. "Equine Relics of the Civil War." *Southern Cultures, Volume 6, Number 1: Five-Year Anniversary Issue.*

"More Horse Thieves." *The Daily American,* October 7, 1893, page 6.

"Seeking Stolen Property." *The Daily American,* June 15, 1893, page 2.

20. Dead Man Robs Post Office

IT is common for jailed persons, or those about to go to prison, to take their own lives in final acts of desperation. In fact, it happens so often, that few ever question it. This is a story about an instance when neither family members nor law enforcement officials thought to question the suicide of a young criminal.

The story begins on August 31, 1894 when "Pick" Beasley, Newt Reece (a youngster of 16 or 17), and a young woman dressed in men's clothing went to the Red Boiling Springs home of an elderly and feeble man named W. J. Murphy. Murphy lived near Red Boiling Springs.

The trio lured Murphy to his front door, and one of them struck him in the face with a rock. They then forced the dazed man back inside his house and tortured him by holding him over a fire until he relented and told them where he kept his lifesavings hidden.

The villains took all Murphy's money (more than $100) and then for no reason except sheer meanness, they burned all Murphy's notes and papers. The malicious threesome promised the old man that if he reported the robbery they would return and kill him.

Murphy did not remain silent. He informed the authorities and they rounded up Reece and the woman quickly and lodged them in the county jail at Lafayette. The woman claimed to be Pick Beasley's wife. In truth, she did live with Beasley, but the two were never married legally.

Pick Beasley was not with the other two robbers when the authorities arrested them. He had abandoned them and gone into hiding in Kentucky. Beasley dodged authorities for some time, but he could not avoid apprehension forever. Eventually, he found himself under arrest and in jail in Lafayette. After spending some time in confinement, Beasley evidently made bond, left jail, and moved in with some of his relatives in Smith County.

With his trial date fast approaching, Beasley was despondent. He knew he would have to return to Macon County and face certain conviction, or he would have to go on the run again and remain a fugitive until recaptured. Then, he hit upon desperate plan to avoid justice.

Pick Beasley walked to the mouth of Peyton's Creek near a deep, deep sinkhole on Jerome Beasley's farm. There, Pick penned a long suicide note and addressed it to his father. In the sad note, Beasley apologized and asked his family not to grieve for him. Pick then attached the note to a bush a few feet from the gaping sinkhole.

When Pick's family members found the note, they believed the distraught young man had launched himself down the sinkhole to his demise. With no way to retrieve his body easily, his family declared the sinkhole Pick's grave.

The suicide caused a compassionate stir in the hearts of the community. Most soon forgot the kind of person Pick Beasley really was.

Authorities too bought the idea that Pick Beasley was at the bottom of the sinkhole and dead. They made no investigation into the suicide.

During the night of July 20, 1895, robbers broke into R. H. Cleveland's store at Pleasant Shade in Smith County. The store also served as the local post office and along with the large amount of clothing, money, and other items the thieves took from the store, they also robbed the post office of a number of stamps.

Stealing the stamps was a serious blunder. It allowed Cleveland to exercise his police powers as a postmaster. Cleveland organized a posse and scoured the area for the culprits. Since robbing a post office is a federal offense, Cleveland had the authority to cross the Smith County line in search of his prey.

On July 27, after a week of sporadic searching, Cleveland and his men came across tracks in the deep woods of eastern Macon County. The tracks led to a cedar thicket where the two robbers had made their camp.

Although they tried to move quietly, Cleveland and his men did not surprise the bandits. When they saw the posse coming, the felons rode away on their mules as quickly as they could. Seeing they were about to lose their prey, posse members opened fire on the pair of criminals. One of the robbers suffered a gunshot wound and the posse followed the blood trail for some time before they lost it. Cleveland surmised that the robbers had escaped into Kentucky.

While Cleveland didn't catch the post office bandits, he did get close enough to them to make positive identifications. One was 16-year-old Will Brown. The boy came from a good family in Pleasant Shade. The other culprit was the supposed dead man, Pick Beasley!

Their embarrassment at falling for Beasley's suicide hoax notwithstanding, the authorities continued to pursue him. They eventually captured Beasley and Brown. They housed Beasley in jail at Hartsville, and transported Brown to Carthage and jailed him there.

On August 20, 1895, after a hearing lasting two days, United States Commissioner R. C. Williams bound Will Brown over for trial in Federal Court for robbing the post office at Pleasant Shade. The Commissioner decided to allow local officials to dispose of their cases against Beasley before binding him over for trial in Federal Court.

This strange, strange case took another wild twist on the evening of October 10, 1895 when Will Brown escaped from the jail at Carthage.

Brown had developed a dangerously high fever in September 1895 that left the young man bedridden for almost a month. The Sheriff of Smith County, who also acted as the county jailer, had isolated Brown in a section of the facility alone and had a nurse by the name of George Bates to "wait on" the segregated prisoner.

On the night of August 20, the Sheriff allowed Brown, who had only recently regained the ability to walk, and Bates to remain in the corridor outside Brown's cell. The Sheriff locked the door leading from the corridor to the remainder of the jail. Then, as left for the evening, the Sheriff locked the stockade surrounding the jail as well.

When the Sheriff returned the next morning, he found the jail unlocked and Brown gone. The Sheriff was certain that Brown had benefitted from outside help. He surmised that friends had let Brown out of jail and then had spirited him away. After all, it was not Brown's first escape attempt. About six weeks earlier, Brown's father had tried to spring his son. The elder Brown went to jail for his trouble.

Brown did not remain free for long. For all Brown's efforts to avoid justice, the Smith County Sheriff recaptured him and returned him to jail.

On April 1, 1896, Pick Beasley and Will Brown finally went on trial for robbing R. H. Cleveland's store. The trial concluded on April 4. The jury found both defendants guilty and sentenced them to three years each in the state penitentiary at Nashville.

In another twist, the District Attorney General revealed that he had made a previous bargain with the accused and he had promised them that they would only receive sentences of two years each. The judge overruled the jury and allowed the plea bargain to stand.

Pick Beasley did not serve his full two years in prison. Despite Beasley's utter disregard for the law and the property of others, on May 7, 1897, Governor Robert Love Taylor pardoned him.

Sources.

"Commissioners Meet." *The Nashville American*, May 8, 1897, page 5.

"Finally Got His Dues. *The Nashville American*, October 12, 1895, page 1.

"News in the State." *The Daily American*, September 4, 1894, page 8.

"Post Office Robber." *The Nashville American*, August 22, 1895, page 1.

"Up to His Old Tricks." *The Nashville American*, July 31, 1895, page 3.

"Williams Gives Bond." *The Nashville American*, April 8, 1896, page 4.

21. Obnoxious Man Beaten

WHEN people get drunk and cause problems, they often encounter trouble they don't bargain for. Sometimes that trouble leads to serious consequences, or even tragedy. Such was the case with a Macon County man named Joe Pierson in the springtime of 1897.

On April 29, 1897, a very drunken Joe Pierson was driving his wagon through Hartsville on his way back to his home in Lafayette. He was in a surly mood and he was evidently sporting for trouble. Pierson stopped his wagon near a group of people and – perhaps on purpose – dropped his horsewhip. He then he ordered an African American child to pick the whip up and hand it to him.

An African American man named Dero Burrow wanted to shield the child from what a potentially dangerous situation. Burrow told the youngster not to retrieve the whip. With that, an enraged Pierson began cursing Burrow.

Becoming angry himself, Burrow told Pierson to stop cursing him and to go on his way. Instead of doing the sensible thing and moving on, the drunken Pierson only intensified his cursing and slurring Burrow.

Finally, Burrow became so angry at the verbal abuse that he picked up a rock and a stick and beat the drunken troublemaker senseless. Burrow did not stop pounding upon

Pierson's head until the drunken troublemaker was unconscious and in critical condition.

Shortly after the incident, the Trousdale County Sheriff arrested and jailed Burrow. A Justice of the Peace scheduled Burrow's trial for May 3, 1897.

Source.

"Beaten Into Insensibility." *The Nashville American*, May 1, 1897, page 24.

22. Stray Bullet Injures Horse

As unfortunate as it was, violent altercations between whites and African Americans were all too commonplace in 19th Century America. Macon County was no exception. One such altercation took place in mid October 1898.

An African American man named John Knapp was walking along the road near Stewart's General Store in the Hughes community (Gravel Hill) of western Macon County. Knapp came upon two white men. Alison Templeton and his brother were traveling on horseback in the opposite direction.

The Templeton's were blocking Knapp's way, or at least he thought they were, and he demanded that they let him pass. When the Templetons did not move, Knapp threatened to shoot them.

The argument continued for several minutes and one can imagine what words passed between Knapp and the Templeton brothers. Finally, Knapp pulled his single-shot pistol and fired at Alison Templeton. The round missed Templeton, but struck his brother's horse in the neck.

Knapp fled and Alison Templeton gave chase, but could not catch him. A manhunt got underway immediately for Knapp.

As it turned out, the gunshot wound did not injure the horse seriously and it survived.

Source.

"Negro Desperado." *The Nashville American*, October 14, 1898, page 6.

23. Shootout at Social Event

MACON County, Tennessee was not part of the Old West geographically, but it certainly had it share of bloody brawls and deadly shootouts.

During the evening of August 16, 1902, there was a social gathering in Macon County's Hillsdale community given for, and attended by, African Americans. At some point, a disturbance broke out. Angry words soon turned into a fiercely violent free-for-all. Participants battled with everything from knuckles to rocks and sticks. Then, the melee turned deadly.

After engaging in fisticuffs for some time, Virgil Sullivan and Jim Jones escalated their personal war. Each man drew his revolver and opened fire. A bullet entered Sullivan's right side, passed through his body, and exited the other side causing massive damage. Jones suffered wounds to his hand and the left side of his body. The attending physician expected both men to die within hours or days.

Source.

"Both Will Die." *The Nashville American*, August 19, 1902, page 5.

24. A $5 Bribe Offer

THROUGHOUT the years, many residents of the rural areas surrounding Davidson County have moved to Nashville and joined the police force there. Several natives of Macon County have had long and successful careers serving as cops in Nashville. A few have even risen to high-ranking positions within the force.

This is the story of a young man from Macon County that wanted badly to serve the citizens of Nashville. He was even willing to break the law for the chance.

On November 3, 1902, a slender young man ambled into the office of Nashville Chief of Police Henry Curran. The man, who said he hailed from Macon County, struck quite a figure. He wore bright green pants, a shiny blue coat and a blue vest covered with brass buttons.

The bold young man smiled and said to the Chief, "My name is Bertle Gass, and I want to get on the police force." Without taking a breath he continued, "I am six feet tall, weigh 180 pounds, and can hit the bull's eye every time with a rifle."

Gass amused the Chief, but he interviewed the out of place applicant anyway. Curran began, "We stopped carrying rifles here last week. We use big pistols now. Can you do any good with a pistol?"

Bertle Gass, exuding confidence, answered truthfully, "No, sir, I never did shoot a pistol none, but I'll practice up with one and I guess I'll be all right in two or three days, won't I?"

Chief Curran nodded and said he thought that with a little practice Gass would do okay with a pistol. The Chief then looked at the skinny young man and asked, "By the way, you say you weigh 180 pounds?"

Gass replied, "Yes, sir." Then trying to convince the Chief he really was as heavy as he said he was, Gass said, "I'm the deceivinest you every saw about my weight."

"Do you belong to a church?" The Chief asked. "All our policemen have to belong to a church. It's one of our rules."

The confidence drained from the young man for a few seconds, then he brightened and asked, "Would it be all right if I joined by Sunday?"

"Yes, I guess it would do," replied the Chief.

Chief Curran continued, "There is another thing. Are you married?"

"No, sir, I ain't married, but my girl up at Salt Lick said she'd hook up with me if I got on the force."

The Chief grimaced and said to Gass, "Well, all policemen have to be married. You'll have to be married first before you can be a policeman."

The young man fancied himself a problem solver. After a few seconds thought, Gass said to the Chief, "Well, I'll write to her and maybe she'll marry me to help me get the job."

Then, the applicant had a question. "Do you reckon there's any chance to get on in the next three months?"

"Well, yes," replied Chief Curran, "there might be a vacancy in the next two or three days."

Gass smiled with relief and told the Chief, "I was going to Texas to work on a farm, but if I can get on in three months I'll stay here. Being on the police force will beat farming won't it?"

The Chief agreed that law enforcement was a better career than working as a hired hand on a farm was.

Then, Gass attempted to make it worth the Chief's while to hire him. "Well, I'll be willing to give you $5 if I can get the job," the young man said.

Chief Curran smiled broadly at the tiny bribe offer and told the young man that he would be in touch.

Gass thought the interview had gone well. He sauntered out of the Chief's office believing he would soon be wearing the blue uniform of Nashville's finest.

Sources.

"Henry Curran, Former Chief of Police, Is Dead." *The Nashville Tennessean*, February 3, 1929, pages 1,5.

"Liberal Yoeman." *The Nashville American*, November 4, 1902, page 2.

25. Three Killed at Dance

SOCIAL events, as popular as they are among the fun loving crowd, sometimes turn tragic. Such was the case in late July, 1903.

There was a well-attended summertime dance in Macon County and most of the attendees wanted nothing more than to have a good time. Sadly, the event soon turned savage, brutal, and tragic.

During the evening, the beauty of a young woman named Julia Bell attracted the attention of several of the young men there. However, she spent most of her time on the dance floor with a handsome young man called Jim Frets. A large number of those rejected by Bell became jealous of Frets. Eventually, a gang of seven men attacked him.

The seven attackers inflicted deep cuts on the head and face of their victim. Bell tried to intervene on the behalf of Frets, and she suffered a minor cut to one of her arms.

Believing he was in a life and death struggle. Frets finally drew his six-shooter and emptied it at his assailants. When Frets stopped shooting, three people were on the floor dead and a fourth had suffered critical wounds. The other three attackers ran away without suffering injury.

The dead included Tom Fields, Clay House, and Dick Mason. Authorities identified the seriously wounded man as Mike Johnson.

Source.

"Killed Three Men." *The Nashville American*, July 26, 1903, page 4.

26. Illegal Telephone Service?

Too often, we assume that what we read and hear coming from the media is accurate, even though we know that sometimes it isn't. Inaccurate media reports are nothing new. This chapter looks at a newspaper article from 1904 accusing a Macon County business of wrongdoing and the attempt by the company President to set the record straight.

Telephone service was still relatively new to rural America in the first years of the 20th Century. Since the technology then was nothing like it is today, it was possible for clever individuals to tap into telephone lines and to pirate phone service free of charge. Moreover, a large number of "wildcat" telephone companies operated for long periods without paying any fees or taxes on their operations.

In those days, the Tennessee Railroad Commission regulated telephone service in the Volunteer State and they worked with the State Comptroller's Office to locate wildcat telephone businesses. On April 2, 1904, *The Nashville American* reported that in March of that year, the State Comptroller, a man named Dribble, discovered an illegal telephone operation headquartered in Lafayette. The paper reported that the name of the service was the "Union Telephone Company."

Dribble said he learned that Union Telephone had strung seventy-five miles of phone lines and had operated for more than two years without paying any taxes or fees.

One might assume that state authorities would have ordered the wildcat telephone company shut down, and had Union Telephone Company executives arrested and jailed, but that didn't happen. Telephone service was too important to the progress of the state to tear down seventy-five miles of line and cut off phone service to hundreds of households. Instead, according to the newspaper, the state mailed the Union Telephone Company a bill for the back taxes and fees it owed, along with a rate schedule so it could operate legally in the future.

That isn't where the story ends. Union Telephone Company President W. H. Carter reacted strongly to the reports that his was a wildcat company. In a letter to *The Nashville American* dated April 5, 1904, Carter wrote that the Union Telephone Company was "respectable and legitimate." Carter even offered proof that his company operated legally. He contended that he could produce receipts of payments made by Union Telephone to a state tax collector named Theodore F. King.

The Nashville American printed Carter's letter, but it didn't offer any kind of retraction or apology for its previous story.

Sources.

"Holds King's Receipts." *The Nashville American*, April 7, 1906, page 7.

"'Wildcat' Telephone Line." *The Nashville American*, April 2, 1904, page 6.

27. A Fowl Dispute and a Killing

NEIGHBORS don't always get along. In fact, they often disagree. After weeks or months of back and forth arguments, a minor event can be the spark that ignites a tragic occurrence and leave a neighbor dead.

Herschel Duncan and Albert Jones were neighbors. They lived in southern Macon County near the Trousdale County line. Both of them were from good families. Duncan's father was a former member of the Trousdale County Court and Jones was the son of a well-known peddler in Macon County.

Duncan and Jones had been sniping at each other for some time over petty things. Their disagreements came to a head on Monday, August 21, 1905 over a trivial matter. It seems that some chickens belonging to Jones got onto Duncan's property and Duncan confronted Jones about it.

The minor dispute soon grew into a major argument and an insanely angry Duncan drew his knife. Not a mere threat, Duncan attacked Jones, stabbing him some ten times. One of Duncan's thrusts penetrated deep into his victim's chest, near his heart.

Regardless of the circumstances, Albert Jones suffered a fate that no one deserves to endure. He experienced intense pain with no doctor or any type of painkiller available to relieve his suffering. About thirty minutes after the senseless stabbing, his agony finally ended when Jones expired.

Sources.

"News Summary." *The Nashville American*, August 23, 1905, page 1.

"Stabbed to Death." *The Nashville American*, August 23, 1905, page 1.

28. An Unhappy Record

MACON County, Tennessee developed the well-earned reputation of being a place where crime, although sometimes notorious, was rare. There were been periods in the county's history that challenged that reputation, however.

In late March 1906, a Macon County Grand Jury met and disposed of a remarkably crowded docket. By the time it closed shop, the diligent Grand Jury members had established a sad record. No Grand Jury in the county's history had ever returned more indictments ("True Bills") or indicted more individuals during a single term before.

By the time the Grand Jury finished its business, it had named some 112 individuals in 72 separate indictments. The number of indictments was staggering when one considers that the 112 accused represented almost one percent of the county's total population.

Most of those indicted were not violent criminals. The bulk of them were moonshiners and others involved in the illicit liquor trade then flourishing in Macon County. While most citizens were willing to tolerate the bootleggers, the Grand Jury was not. Evidently, they saw it as their duty to stamp out the illegal liquor operations in their county.

The regular session of the Circuit Court presided over by Judge Hull was also busy dealing with moonshiners. The District Attorney General was very aggressive in his prosecutions and he managed to win convictions in four separate cases against moonshiners during the Circuit Court's term.

Sources.

Forstall, Richard L. (editor). *Population of Counties by Decennial Census: 1900-1990.* Washington D. C.: US Census Bureau, 1995.

"Macon County Grand Jury Breaks Records." *The Nashville American*, March 27, 1906.

29. Macon Sheriff Arrested

No one, regardless of station, is above the law. Even those that carry badges sometimes find that the law applies to them as well as it does everyone else.

Macon County Sheriff James Ragland was a large man, and at 37-years-old, a youthful one. Ragland was no prohibitionist. In fact, he was a drinking man, and he made some of the same mistakes that drinkers often make.

On the evening of January 21, 1908, Ragland was on Nashville's Fourth Avenue. He had been drinking heavily and there was some sort of altercation between him and another man.

Two Nashville patrol officers came upon Ragland and the other man, and an argument soon ensued between them and the Sheriff. Eventually, the police saw no other recourse except to arrest the rowdy Sheriff. The officers relieved Ragland of his pistol, hauled him to the Davidson County jail, and charged him with drunk and disorderly conduct.

The arrest didn't damage Ragland's good reputation with the citizens of Macon County and he won reelection in 1908 and 1910 by running on his record. During the 1910 campaign, the Sheriff's supporters claimed proudly, "Mr. Ragland has caught more hardened criminals and let fewer get away than any other Sheriff of Macon County since the war."

Sources.

Blankenship, Harold G. *History of Macon County, Tennessee.* Tompkinsville, Kentucky: Monroe County Press, 1986, page 155.

Gammon, CL. *Revenue Raiders: Macon County's Whiskey War.* Lafayette, Tennessee: Deep Read Press, 2022, page 69.

"Hustling for Votes in Macon." *The Nashville American*, December 5, 1909, page 16.

"Sheriff Locked Up." *The Nashville American*, January 21, 1908, page 2.

30. Henry Crook Kills Again

CHAPTER 17 detailed Henry Crook's murder of his landlord, William Burrow. Sixteen years later, Crook made news again – this time for killing his nephew.

The tragedy took place at the home of Jeff Gann on September 8, 1908. The victim was the Gann's seven-year-old son, Pattie. The strange story was that three of Gann's sons were standing in the doorway of their house and the oldest fired two rounds from a revolver at a tree. Then, as the boys turned to reenter the home, the youngest, Pattie, screeched out in pain and said he was "hurt." The boy staggered a few steps into the house and then fell to the floor dead.

The examining physician found that a single bullet had entered Pattie's body just below his left shoulder blade and had proceeded to pierce his heart. The victim's brothers told Sheriff Ragland that they didn't hear the shot that killed their brother, but neighbors heard the report of a rifle immediately after the boy fired at the tree with his pistol.

Suspicion fell on Henry Crook. Crook proclaimed his innocence, but his statement didn't exactly clear him. Crook admitted he was hunting within a few hundred yards of the Gann home on the day of the killing. He further admitted that he took a shot at a hawk at about the same time the boy suffered his mortal wound. However, Crook contended that if he did shoot the boy it was accidental. Crook offered the theory that his bullet might have ricocheted off a tree and hit the boy.

While the evidence of intentional homicide was weak, Sheriff Ragland took Crook into custody anyway.

Sources.

Gann, Pattie. *Tennessee Death Records, 1908-1965*. Nashville, Tennessee: Tennessee State Library and Archives.

"Murder of Nephew." *The Nashville American*, September 8, 1908, page 2.

31. Man Mistaken for Bear

BOOTLEGGERS were so common in Macon County in the early 20th Century that most citizens, drinkers or not, accepted them. While law enforcement agents arrested bootleggers often, they tended to treat them decently.

Although he was only 26, Thomas Andrews had been involved in the bootlegging trade in both Tennessee and across the line in Kentucky for several years. During its previous session, the Macon County Grand Jury indicted Andrews for selling whiskey to a minor. In order to avoid arrest, Andrews skipped over the border into Kentucky and got away.

Andrews continued plying his trade while in Bluegrass State. When Kentucky authorities began to bear down on him, Andrews slipped back across the line and surrendered to Macon County authorities. Then, while Andrews awaited trial on the first charge, another Grand Jury indicted him on two counts of selling liquor inside the Macon County Courthouse. A jury convicted Andrews on all three counts and Judge Joseph M. Gardenhire sentenced him to jail.

As already illustrated, Macon County Sheriff James Ragland was not offended by the illicit alcohol trade. Andrews had a wife and five children and on the morning of December 25, 1908, the compassionate Sheriff agreed to allow the bootlegger to go home to celebrate the Christmas holiday with his family, provided he returned to the jail afterward.

Andrews did not keep his word to the Sheriff. Instead of going home, he spent the day drinking with friends. About 7 o'clock that evening, Andrews staggered to the house of a widow named Coley and collapsed on her doorstep in a drunken stupor. It was a very cold evening and Andrews had cinched the collar of his long, thick buffalo overcoat around his face.

Andrews snored so loudly that it aroused the attention of the people inside. Widow Coley thought the sounds on the porch might be coming from a growling animal. Unsure, she sent her young son to see what was causing the racket. The boy went to the door and called out. When there was no answer, the boy cracked the door open and looked out into the growing darkness to see what was outside. Startled, the boy hastened to slam the door shut.

Hurrying back to his mother, the Coley boy said to her, "It's a bear, or something, with long wool all over it."

Now very worried, the woman asked a visiting neighbor if he would go to the door and see what was outside. The man, a farmer named Thomas Decker, picked up his shotgun and went to the door. Fearing that a vicious beast might attack him, he very cautiously opened the door a few inches and peered out.

The man could not make out for sure what he was looking at, so he poked the figure with his gun barrel and called out to it. The only answer he received was a snoring sound he mistook for growling. Decker poked the figure again and asked for a response. There was none.

The man poked what he now believed to be a bear for a third time and demanded it go away. When there was no movement from the figure, Decker fired his shotgun at pointblank range, killing Andrews instantly.

On the afternoon of December 26, a Coroner's Jury held an Inquest and determined that the killing of Andrews was justified. There was some talk that a Grand Jury should at least review the facts in the case, but there was no paperwork filed in that regard.

Sources.

Andrews, Thomas. *Tennessee Death Records, 1908-1965*. Nashville, Tennessee: Tennessee State Library and Archives.

Gammon, CL. *Revenue Raiders: Macon County's Whiskey War*. Lafayette, Tennessee: Deep Read Press, 2022, pages 71-73

"Very Unusual Sort of Killing." *The Nashville American*, December 27, 1908, page 2.

32. Murder on the Square, Again

MURDER, it seems, can happen anywhere, at any time. The Public Square at Lafayette was the scene of another killing two days after the national Thanksgiving celebration of 1909.

A little before 7 o'clock on the evening of November 27, 1909, Dr. William E. King rode astride his horse in front of the building housing the newly established Citizen's Bank on the Lafayette Public Square. The doctor was a youthful 37, and until recently, he had been successful and well respected. But a dispute had damaged his practice and had cost him many friends. On this evening, it is likely that the dispute cost Dr. King his life.

As Dr. King rode along, a loud report from a gun jarred the quiet autumn evening. The blast blew King from his horse and he crashed hard to the street. Then, the assassin ran up to the badly wounded man and fired two more bullets into the doctor's head. King died instantly.

Few people were on the Public Square at the time of the shooting and no one admitted witnessing it. Yet, strong suspicion fell upon a former teller of Citizen's Bank named Albert Dean. Dean and King had been close friends and King was the Dean family physician for a considerable time.

In 1908, Dean and his wife separated. The rumor was that that the breakup occurred because Dr. King had engaged in "improper relations" with Dean's spouse.

The friendship was shattered and Dean and King became bitter enemies. King had even left Macon County for several weeks to avoid Dean, but he had returned.

The belief that Albert Dean had killed Dr. King caused the authorities to act. Warrants ordered Dean's arrest, but he was not immediately located.

From the outset, the case promised to be sensational. Macon County citizens disagreed strongly with each other about the case. One camp held that Dean had murdered the doctor and that he deserved severe punishment for his crime. The other camp, including Dean's many friends in Macon County and the surrounding area, held that the former bank teller was innocent. Even if Dean had committed the killing, according to Dean's friends, he had given King what he deserved.

On the morning of December 9, 1908, Smith County Sheriff B. M. Dean took the suspect into custody. The Sheriff then contacted his counterpart in Macon County and informed him that Albert Dean was under arrest. By noontime, Macon County Sheriff James Ragland had traversed the twenty odd miles from Lafayette to Carthage with a warrant from a Macon County Justice of the Peace allowing him to take the suspect into custody.

When Ragland got to Carthage, he learned that Albert Dean had hired attorneys and they had started the legal maneuvering. As he arrived at the Smith County jail, someone handed Sheriff Ragland a writ of *habeas corpus*. The writ ordered Ragland to take the prisoner to the Smith County courthouse for a hearing before Judge Joseph M. Gardenhire.

Dean's attorneys claimed their client was innocent and that he was entitled to bail. They also stated that they feared that Dr. King's friends would attack Dean if Sheriff Ragland took him back to Lafayette for a preliminary hearing.

Judge Gardenhire scheduled the *habeas corpus* hearing for December 16, and then he ordered the defendant lodged in the Smith County jail until then.

The District Attorney General had to know he had a difficult task ahead of him in prosecuting Dean. The defendant had hired a formidable defense team consisting of John S. Wooten of Lafayette, Ed Foust of Hartsville, and Carthage attorneys W. V. Lee and L. A. Ligon.

On December 16, Judge Gardenhire held the *habeas corpus* hearing on schedule. Dean's attorneys requested bail for their client and the District Attorney General did not oppose it, provided that the bond be at least the agreed upon sum of $15,000.

The judge agreed to the bond and ordered Dean to appear before the next session of the Circuit Court in Lafayette.

Although the bail was substantial, Dean had no trouble making it. Thirty-three well-to-do citizens of Macon, Smith, Trousdale, and other Tennessee counties signed Dean's bond.

Dean was all smiles and he exuded confidence during the hearing. His confidence had to grow as he left the courtroom and scores of well-wishers patted him on the back and shook his hand.

Sources:

"A. R. Dean Charged with Murder of Dr. W. E. King." *The Nashville Tennessean*, December 11, 1909, page 10.

"Assassinated on the Public Square." *The Nashville Tennessean*, November 30, 1909, page 5.

"Charged With Murder of Dr. W. E. King." The Nashville Tennessean, December 11, 1909, page 7.

"Dr. W. E. King Shot from His Horse at Lafayette." *The Nashville American*, November 28, 1909, page 1.

King, Dr. William E. *Tennessee Death Records, 1908-1965*. Nashville, Tennessee: Tennessee State Library and Archives.

Taft, William A. Proclamation 883—Thanksgiving Day, 1909. The American Presidency Project.

33. A Bail Jumper Kidnapped

WE have all read stories and seen movies about bounty hunters in the pay of bondsmen, and sometimes the bondsmen themselves, brutalizing bail jumpers while bringing them to justice. Naturally, sometimes the tables are turned. Such a case took place in 1910.

On March 3, 1910, Isaac Beasley of Macon County, a professional bail bondsman, found himself under arrest in Monroe County, Kentucky. The charge was kidnapping a man named Homer Dyer.

Dyer had committed a misdemeanor in Macon County and legal authorities there indicted and convicted him of it. The judge ordered Dyer to pay a fine by a given date or to serve a jail term.

Dyer contacted Beasley and Beasley secured Dyer's bond. Then, Dyer crossed the state line into Kentucky and out of the jurisdiction of Tennessee. It was clear that Dyer intended to stay in Kentucky and avoid paying the fine.

A few days before Dyer was to go to court and pay his fine, Beasley went on Monroe County and begged Dryer to return Tennessee with him. Beasley explained that unless Dyer came back and made the fine good, that the court would forfeit the bond and Beasley would have to pay it.

Dyer didn't care that he was leaving Beasley on the hook for the bond. He flatly refused to return to Macon County and face up to his obligation. Beasley felt he had no other choice except to bring Dyer back by force. Beasley arrested Dyer and started the journey to Lafayette, but before they crossed the state line, Dyer escaped from Beasley. Then, Dyer went to the Monroe County authorities and swore out a warrant against Beasley charging him with kidnapping.

Kentucky authorities had no choice but to arrest Beasley and lodge him in the Monroe County jail at Glasgow. Ironically, Beasley had to make bond or remain in jail until a Monroe County Grand Jury could sort out the confusing case. He chose to make bond.

Source.

"Tried to Carry His Bondsman to Tennessee." *The Nashville Tennessean*, March 5, 1910, page 1.

34. Murder at Highland School

BLOOD feuds, though we seldom call them that, are more common, even today, than one might suppose. A particularly bloody fight between feuding parties took place in Macon County in 1910.

The Highland schoolhouse a few miles from Lafayette hosted Sunday school on June 19, 1910. Nothing happened during the service that indicated what was about to happen.

Sunday school ended at about 4 p.m., and mere minutes later, twenty-five to thirty gunshots rang out from a wheat field across the road from the school. When the shooting stopped, several who heard the gunfire hurried to the wheat field and found a grotesque scene.

Eighteen-year-old Lonzo Gann, the son of Joe Gann, was dead from the three bullet wounds – one to his neck and two to his body. Robert Nichols received three leg wounds. One lead ball entered his thigh and lodged in his femur.

Arch Parker was a highly respected resident living in Hartsville. Four of Parker's sons were involved in the bloody encounter and two of them received gunshot wounds. Rom Parker received a round to the back that passed completely through his lung. Monk Parker received a thigh wound. The other two Parkers, Archie B. (sometimes called "Arch") and Brink, were not injured during the shootout.

Soon after the shooting, Sheriff James Ragland received a call and he hurried to the scene. He found that the participants in the bloodbath other than those mentioned above were Hat Reeves, a person named Brumitt and another one named Gregory. The Sheriff also learned that at least five members of the feuding factions fired pistols at each other during the several long seconds that lead filled the air.

The case was confusing, but the word was that The Parkers and Lonzo Gann had been feuding for some time. In an earlier altercation, an ally of Gann had stabbed one of the Parkers. After considering the facts, a Grand Jury indicted Archie B., Brink, and Monk Parker for murder.

The Parkers stood trial for the murder of Lonzo Gann on three separate occasions. The first jury convicted them, but Judge Joseph M. Gardenhire ordered a new trial. The second trial jury hung and the judge ordered a mistrial.

The District Attorney was persistent and he prosecuted the Parkers a third time. The trial opened in July 1912 with the prosecutor arguing that the shootout amounted to murder because Brink Parker started it when he opened fire on Lonzo Gann. The prosecutor continued that Gann had tried to run away and it was only after he could not escape that Gann returned fire. The defense countered, saying Gann, not the Parkers, initiated the firefight.

The On July 14, 1912 the jury convicted the Parkers of second-degree murder, and sentenced them to fifteen years each in prison. The three filed appeals and the court granted them bonds of $2,000 each. As soon as the three left the Macon County jail, they fled. Archie B. and Monk Parker headed north to Canada, while Brink Parker went into hiding in Florida.

In January 1913, the Tennessee Supreme Court heard arguments on the appeal of Archie B. and Monk Parker. Since both men were fugitives and did not appear, the High Court rejected their appeals.

On September 25, 1913, word came as to whereabouts of Archie B. Parker. Indisputable evidence placed him in Toronto, Canada. Evidence also indicated that Monk Parker had died in Canada. Macon County officials insisted upon the return of Archie B. Parker to their jurisdiction. Nashville patrol officer, W. D. Beasley left immediately for Canada to retrieve the convicted murderer.

Beasley made it back to Nashville on October 2, with Parker in tow. Parker remained in the jail in Nashville until Macon County Sheriff Johnnie Hanes could pick him up and return him to the jail at Lafayette.

While one of Lonzo Gann's killers was in jail, and one was dead, Brink Parker was still at large.

Archie B. Parker was not willing to serve his time without more maneuvering. In November 1913, he again asked the Supreme Court to hear his appeal. Burned once, Judge Gardenhire did not grant Parker the opportunity to make bond again. Instead, the judge remanded Parker to the Davidson County jail at Nashville for safe keeping."

Archie B. Parker got his appeal before the Tennessee Supreme Court on April 4, 1914. The Tennessee High Court denied Parker's motion for a new trial and ordered him to serve his prison term.

Archie B. Parker did not serve his full sentence. He contracted tuberculosis and in 1917, doctors determined had he had just a short time to live. Judge Gardenhire, the District Attorney, local attorneys, numerous Macon County citizens, and the State Board of Parole all requested a pardon for Parker. They claimed that keeping Parker in jail would only hasten his death. They also pointed out that Parker was only 20, and therefore, a minor, when he killed Lonzo Gann. Finally, they told the Governor that Parker's brother Rom, who lived in Texas, would care for him for the little time he had left.

On October 6, 1917, Governor Thomas C. Rye pardoned Archie B. Parker and ordered him released from prison. Archie B. Parker never made it to Texas, however. He died in Watertown, Tennessee on November 20, 1917.

Although evidence indicated he was on the scene, authorities never charged Rom Parker in the killing of Lonzo Gann. Rom died a hero in combat during World War I.

Brink Parker remained a fugitive until the end of April 1926, when he negotiated his surrender at Nashville. Brink Parker applied for a pardon immediately. Judge Gardenhire and the Attorney General recommended the pardon.

Governor Austin Peay pored over the court record of more than 800 pages. Peay believed the defense contention that Gann started the fight and the Governor felt that the Attorney General should have never prosecuted the Parkers for murder. The Governor's opinions, coupled with the fact that Brink was the only surviving Parker brother, caused Peay to pardon the longtime fugitive. Thus, the Governor ended the sixteen-year-old murder case brought on by a family feud.

Sources.

"Alleged Murderer is Brought Here." *The Nashville Tennessean and the Nashville American*, October 3, 1913, page 1.

"Arch Parker Here." *The Nashville Tennessean and the Nashville American*, November 24, 1913, page 2A.

Blankenship, Harold G. *History of Macon County, Tennessee.* Tompkinsville, Kentucky: Monroe County Press, 1986, page 155.

"By Justice Lansdon, *The Nashville Tennessean and the Nashville American*, January, 1913, page 2A.

"Convicted of Murder." *The Nashville Tennessean and the Nashville American*, July 25, 1912, page 12.

"Domestic." *The Nashville American*, June 20, 1910, page 1.

"Fugitive for Years, who Surrendered, Pardoned by Peay." *The Nashville Tennessean*, May 13, 1926, pages 1, 3.

"Macon County Tragedy." *The Nashville American*, June 21, 1910, page 4.

"One Killed and Three Wounded in Pistol Fight." *The Nashville Tennessean*, June 21, 1910, page 1.

"Pardon Granted to Macon County Man." *The Nashville Tennessean and the Nashville American*, October 7, 1917, page 12.

Parker, Archie B. *Tennessee Death Records, 1908-1965*. Nashville, Tennessee: Tennessee State Library and Archives.

"Parker Brothers on Trial." *The Nashville Tennessean and the Nashville American*, July 24, 1912, page 7.

"Participants in Macon County Shooting Mum." *The Nashville American*, June 22, 1910, page 2.

Scott, Betty C. Meadows, *Macon County, Tennessee Obituaries and Articles Volume 1*. Lafayette, Tennessee: Ridge Runner Publications and Genealogy Research, 2003, page 47.

"Supreme Court Clears Docket." *The Nashville Tennessean and the Nashville American*, April 5, 1914, page 7.

35. The Cigar Wrapper Shooting

DESPITE Tennessee's Prohibition law then in effect, those wishing to get drunk could usually find a way. On Saturday, July 22, 1911, Marlin Maxey of Red Boiling Springs purchased a large amount of whiskey and got very drunk. Then, he spent much of that evening trying to start a fight with Max Jordan, also of Red Boiling Springs.

Jordan considered Maxey to be a friend of his and he tried avoid trouble with the drunken man. However, Maxey refused to allow Jordan to dissuade him.

Finally, at about 10:30 that night, Maxey attacked Jordan because of a cigar wrapper. Given no choice, Jordan felt forced to act in his own self-defense. Jordan shot his friend twice. One round grazed Maxey's forehead and the other hit him in the hip. Thankfully, neither wound proved fatal.

When Maxey sobered up, he admitted that the altercation was his fault, and he refused to press charges against Jordan.

Sources.

Gammon, CL. *Revenue Raiders: Macon County's Whiskey War*. Lafayette, Tennessee: Deep Read Press, 2022, pages 76-77.

"Shot at Red Boiling Springs." *The Nashville American*, July 25, 1911, page 4.

36. Murder at the County Fair

THE Macon County Fair is a major event each year. There is always a carnival atmosphere complete with amusement park rides, hotdogs, cotton candy, funnel cakes, and other such fare. However, the heart and soul of the county fair is the exhibits of various crops and arts, and crafts. As much as the county fair is a part of the fabric of the community, it has something of a checkered past.

The county fair suffered a tragedy on Friday, August 22, 1913. On that otherwise pleasant summer evening, a man named Charlie Jones shot Deputy Sheriff John Bowman to death during a bloody confrontation.

The deadly encounter began when a drunken Sam Jones and Fred Armistead got into a fight. Special Deputies John Bowman and Harvey Jones went to the scene to break up the altercation.

Sam's brother, Charlie Jones may also have been drunk. Charlie became enraged at the deputies, drew his revolver, and opened fire. One round struck Deputy Bowman in the chest, and another entered his side. After Bowman fell to the ground, Charlie stood over him and shot him in the head killing him instantly.

Charlie Jones also shot Deputy Jones, wounding him seriously. One bullet struck Deputy Jones in the left arm, splintering a bone. Another bullet entered the Deputy Jones near his left hip and lodged deeply in his back muscles. Deputy Jones fired once, striking Sam Jones in the leg, without doing much damage.

His weapon empty, Charlie Jones attempted to escape. He ran to the other side of the fairgrounds where Sheriff Johnnie Hanes captured and arrested him. After Sheriff Hanes took him into custody, Charlie bragged, "If my ammunition hadn't given out, I would have killed the whole bunch."

The shooting did not put a damper on the county fair. The night of the shooting, about 1,500 attended, but the next night the crowds ballooned to around 2,500.

The Jones brothers went before Justice of the Peace M. B. Freeman for a preliminary hearing at 1 o'clock on the afternoon on August 26. Charlie stood charged with first-degree murder. Sam, whom witnesses accused of urging Charlie to shoot Deputy Bowman, faced charges of being an accessory before the fact. Charlie Jones claimed self-defense and Sam entered a plea of not guilty.

Charlie Jones was an ex-convict and many that knew him considered him a dangerous man. A witness testified that a short time before the gunfire started, Charlie Jones told him that Deputies Bowman and Harvey Jones had been watching him all day and that he had warned them to stop following him.

Another witness swore that as Bowman was prostrate on the ground, Sam Jones told Charlie that the deputy was still alive and he encouraged Charlie to finish off Bowman, which Charlie did.

Justice Freeman had more than enough evidence to bind the Jones brothers over for trial at the next session of the Circuit Court in Lafayette. He also denied the two men bond.

Justice Freeman took note of the fact that some elements of the community had promised to form a lynch mob, drag the Jones brothers out of jail, and hang them from the nearest tree. As a precaution, Freeman ordered Sheriff Hanes to transport the brothers to Nashville and have authorities there jail them for safekeeping.

The Jones brothers went on trial at 8 o'clock on the morning of November 20, 1913. There was a circus atmosphere surrounding the proceedings and a huge crowd turned out to see it.

There was no question as to the fact that Charlie Jones killed John Bowman. The case hinged on whether Jones could prove his act was justified.

Deputy Harvey Jones was the prosecution's first witness. He confirmed his previous statements by telling the jury that just before the shooting Sam Joes had an altercation with Fred Armstead. The Deputy continued that he and Deputy Bowman went to the scene to settle the dispute. Sam Jones had a rock in his pocket that he refused to relinquish. But Jones did agree to go away and not cause any more trouble.

Just as it appeared that the deputies had settled the matter, Charlie Jones appeared on the scene. Wishing to avoid another ugly argument, Deputy Bowman turned and began to walk away, but the Jones brothers followed closely behind him. They caught up with Bowman and stepped around in front of him. Charlie Jones screeched at Bowman, "Don't follow me!" Then, Charlie drew his pistol and opened fire. Badly wounded, Bowman fell to the ground. Charlie then turned and shot Deputy Jones.

With Deputy Jones incapacitated, Sam Jones, who was still near the prostrate John Bowman, called out to Charlie, "Come back and shoot this other son of a bitch; he is not dead."

Calmly, Charlie Jones walked back to the helpless Bowman, stood over him, and put a bullet in his brain.

The prosecution called four additional witnesses that confirmed the story related by Deputy Jones.

The defense didn't have much of a case. They attempted to show mitigation by claiming the defendants were too drunk to act rationally.

The case went to the jury on November 22, at about 4 o'clock that afternoon. The jury was not out long before returning guilty verdicts against both defendants.

The Jones brothers requested that Judge Gardenhire grant them new trials. Judge Gardenhire heard arguments on the subject on November 23.

Gardenhire awarded Sam Jones a new trial. He believed that the evidence indicated Sam was obviously too drunk at the time of the slaying to think rationally. Gardenhire ordered Sam taken to Nashville and confined in the Davidson County jail until his next trial.

Gardenhire did not grant Charlie Jones a new trial. On the contrary, the judge sentenced Charlie to suffer death by execution on the day after Christmas, 1913. Gardenhire ordered Charlie held on Death Row in the Tennessee State Prison at Nashville until his execution.

Charlie's attorneys filed an immediate notice of appeal on his behalf. The Tennessee Supreme Court scheduled a ruling on the appeal for mere days before Charlie was to die.

Until 1913, the method of execution in Tennessee was death by hanging. However, that year, the state legislature changed the method to death in the electric chair. Thus, Charlie Jones was to make history by being one of the first Tennessee murderers to die by electrocution.

While Charlie Jones waited for a decision on his appeal, he received some hopeful news. Tennessee prison officials reported that the Kentucky firm from which they had ordered their new $1,750 electric chair was behind schedule in shipping it. Tennessee authorities continued that it might be early 1914 before the chair was ready to fry anyone.

Jones saw his hopes of a delay dashed when the prison engineer J. T. Rushton announced that the new electric would arrive and be operational during the first week in December 1913. Rushton continued that he would place the electric chair in the state penitentiary's "old death-house" where the trapdoor of the gallows was.

While the electric chair did arrive at the prison, Charlie Jones did not sit in it on December 26. The Tennessee Supreme Court overturned his conviction and ordered a new trial for him.

No executions took place in Tennessee between 1913 and 1916. But between 1916 and 1960, the state put 125 persons to death by electrocution. After years of executing murderers by lethal injection, Tennessee resumed death by electrocution in 2007.

The Jones brothers went on trial again on July 27, 1914 and a jury convicted them both again – this time for second-degree murder. Both brothers received long prison sentences.

Sam Jones received a term of 10 to 20 years in prison. Since he had not killed or injured anyone, many felt his sentence was too harsh. Those wanting Sam Jones out of prison started a drive to convince Governor Albert H. Roberts to pardon him.

Governor Roberts considered the situation closely. Because Sam Jones had already served five years in prison, on February 6, 1920, the Governor pardoned him.

Sources.

Blankenship, Harold G. *History of Macon County, Tennessee.* Tompkinsville, Kentucky: Monroe County Press, 1986, pages 125-130, 155.

"Courts in Session in Macon County." *The Nashville, Tennessean and the Nashville American*, July 22, 1914, page 7.

"Electric Chair." *The Nashville, Tennessean and the Nashville American*, December 1, 1913.

"Harve Jones Resting Easy." *The Nashville, Tennessean and the Nashville American*, August 24, 1913, page A3.

"Jones Brothers Are Placed in Local Jail." *The Nashville, Tennessean and the Nashville American*, August 28, 1913, page 1.

"Jones Pardoned." *The Nashville, Tennessean and the Nashville American*, February 7, 1920, page 3.

"Men Accused of Bowman Murder." *The Nashville, Tennessean and the Nashville American*, November 22, 1913, page 14.

"Murder in the First Degree." *The Nashville, Tennessean and the Nashville American*, November 24, 1913, page 1.

"Officers Shot in Macon." *The Nashville, Tennessean and the Nashville American*, August 23, 1913, page 1.

Scott, Betty C. Meadows, *Macon County, Tennessee Obituaries and Articles Volume 1*. Lafayette, Tennessee: Ridge Runner Publications and Genealogy Research, 2003, pages 107, 111, 181.

"Slayers sent to Davidson Jail." *The Nashville, Tennessean and the Nashville American*, August 28, 1913, page 2.

"Tennessee Executions." The Tennessee Department of Corrections website: https://www.tn.gov/correction/statistics-and-information/executions/tennessee-executions.html

37. A Commie in Macon County

FREEDOM of speech is one of America's most cherished liberties. Yet, citizens cannot evoke freedom of speech as an excuse to threaten public safety. As Justice Oliver Wendell Holmes wrote, "The most stringent protection of free speech would not protect a man falsely shouting fire in a theater and causing panic."

Especially during wartime, protecting freedom of speech while providing for national security at the same time is a high-wire act the government tries to perform. Sometimes the government fails to walk the wire.

On April 6, 1917, the United States formally entered World War I. About six weeks later (May 18, 1917), Congress passed the Selective Service Act giving the President the power to draft soldiers into the military.

On June 15, 1917, President Wilson signed the Espionage Act of 1917. The purpose of the law was to prohibit interference with the military or the recruitment of soldiers, to prevent insubordination by soldiers, and to prevent Americans from aiding enemies of the United States during wartime.

As with almost all American conflicts, a large segment of the society opposed the nation's entrance into World War I. Conscripting young men into the service was a cause of disagreement with American leftists, especially the communists. Many on America's leftwing criticized the draft publically and this put them at odds with the laws mentioned above.

Macon County, Tennessee did not avoid the draft controversy or at one visit from a communist. Dr. G. Shell Gregory was a Nashville optometrist and a promoter of the communist agenda.

On the evening of September 8, 1917, members of the Nashville Home Defense League apprehended Gregory and turned him over to a Deputy United States Marshal. Federal authorities charged Gregory with violation of the Selective Service Act and the Espionage Act of 1917. Authorities confined Gregory in the Davidson County jail until he could make a $10,000 bond.

The charges stemmed from a speech Gregory gave before the Framers' Union in Lafayette a few days earlier. During the speech, he expressed his opposition to the draft in very strong terms.

Gregory was a vain man and this made him talkative. He was more than willing to give his side of the story to reporters. Gregory told members of the press that his arrest and confinement were unfair. He contended that he was merely exercising the free speech guaranteed him by the United States Constitution. He denied that he had ever interfered with the draft beyond saying that it was unconstitutional and unjust. He said he grew up in Tennessee and learned that the Constitution was the supreme law of the land.

Gregory continued that he was a socialist and that he had merely repeated the views of the Socialist Party. He repeated that he never urged anyone to violate the draft law, but that he told his audience that they should work to repeal it. He denied that he had ever criticized President Wilson directly. He did admit that he said he believed the administration was unfair.

Gregory continued that he didn't support any side in the war and he was not pro-American. He said that he was not in good standing with the Socialist Party because he opposed the radicalism the party espoused.

Despite what Gregory said, he *was* in good standing with the Socialist Party. After a visit with Gregory, the leader of the Davidson County Socialist Party stated that the eye doctor had expressed the views of the party.

Regardless of Gregory's statement that he had made no statement in violation of the law, federal authorities intended to use the text of his Lafayette speech as evidence against him. Despite the fact that the authorities indicted him, Gregory, after making bail, continued his efforts on the behalf of international communism.

May Day is a day of celebration for the communists. It is not surprising then that Dr. Gregory had another run-in with the law on May Day 1919.

The communists staged a revolution and took charge in Russia in 1917. They then changed the country's name to the Union of Soviet Socialist Republics, stamped out any hope of liberty, and established a totalitarian dictatorship. American communists looked to the Russian communists for guidance and followed the Russian example by calling for a violent overthrow of the American government.

Authorities broke up a communist meeting on a May Day 1919, meeting at Nashville's Ryman Auditorium. The problem centered on a large number of communist pamphlets preaching the violent overthrow of the United States found at the meeting.

It was illegal to distribute materials preaching violence and when the authorities asked rally organizers if they intended to pass out the inflammatory materials to the crowd, the organizers stated "emphatically" that they did. With that, the police ended the rally, cordoned off the building, and dispersed the 250 or so persons in attendance.

Federal agents, Davidson County detectives, and Mayor William Gupton, of Nashville questioned the two men scheduled to be principal speakers at the rally, G. Shell Gregory and Vanderbilt University Professor Russell Scott.

As he always did, Dr. Gregory, who was still under indictment, denied any knowledge of illegal activity. He said he wasn't aware of any communist pamphlets and he condemned the authorities for preventing him from speaking.

Professor Scott denied he was a communist. He told the federal agents that rally organizer Harry Goldfarb asked him to speak. Goldfarb, a Nashville shoemaker, had left the rally as soon as the police arrived. The story was that he went immediately to another rally.

Scott also condemned the authorities for breaking up the rally. He continued that he had moved to the United States from England seven years earlier and that he hoped to be an American citizen soon. Mayor Gupton had nothing but contempt for Scott. The Mayor said that America would be a better place had Scott remained in Europe.

During the original questioning, officials had no evidence that Gregory and Scott had a direct connection to the illegal material. Reluctantly, they released the communist rabble-rousers.

Later revelations connected Scott directly to the illegal communist pamphlets. Scott had passed out some of the material to Vanderbilt students and encouraged them to come to the rally.

Beyond taking part in distributing communist propaganda, Scott had attempted to infiltrate the Vanderbilt R.O.T.C. program with an eye toward damaging the American war effort. U.S. officials called for Scott's ouster from his position at Vanderbilt, but university administrators refused to dismiss him. They said there was no reason to fire Scott because his contract expired in June 1919 anyway.

There was no general amnesty granted to opponents of World War I. However, on December 15, 1923, President Coolidge commuted the sentences of all those convicted for opposing the government and the Selective Service Act during the conflict.

Even after the war, communist sympathizers such as Dr. Gregory continued to agitate for the violent overthrow of the United States even though many of them denied any association with the communists.

Sources:

Ebel, Wilfred L., Lieutenant Colonel, United States Army. "The Amnesty Issue: A Historical Prospective." *Parameters, Volume 4, Number 1.* Washington: United States War College, 1974, pages 66-67.

"Mobilizing for War: The Selective Service Act in World War I." National Archives Website.

Moynihan, Daniel P. *Secrecy: The American Experience.* New Haven, Connecticut: Yale University Press. 1998, page 155.

"Opponent of Draft is Held." *The Nashville, Tennessean and the Nashville American*, September 9, 1917, page 9.

Parker, Richard A. (editor) *Free Speech on Trial: Communication Perspectives on Landmark Supreme Court Decisions.* Tuscaloosa, Alabama: University of Alabama Press, 2003, pages 20–35.

"Scott's Removal Urged by U.S. Authorities." *The Nashville, Tennessean and the Nashville American*, May 3, 1919, page 9.

"U.S. at War with Germany: President Signs Resolution." *Evening Star* (Washington, D. C.), page 1.

U. S. Authorities Break Up Bolshevik Meet Here." *The Nashville, Tennessean and the Nashville American*, May 2, 1919, page 2.

38. A Draft Dodger?

As we saw in the previous chapter, many Americans opposed the draft during World War I, and these people encouraged young men to avoid reporting for duty. Some Americans did fail to report once drafted, but not all of them were trying to shirk military service. Sometimes, they were simply confused as to what the draft notice meant.

All those that didn't answer the call to report for military service automatically received the classification of "deserter." Willie Hix of Macon County's Willette community was one such person. Hix received his draft notice on May 9, 1918, but he didn't report. Rumors spread that Hix went into hiding near his home.

Sheriff Johnny Hanes went to the Hix home, arrested him, and brought him before the local draft board for a hearing on May 27. Hix seemed confused. He told board members that he didn't see any need to report. He assured the board that he wasn't part of any conspiracy and that no one had advised him to dodge the draft.

The draft board determined that Wix was a deserter and that his refusal to report "was willful, malicious, and without good excuse or reason." The board ordered Sheriff Hanes to escort Hix to the nearest camp and hand him over to military authorities.

While there were a few Macon County draftees that did not report for duty, the vast majority did. On May 28 1918, the last 39 of

Macon County's "Class 1" draftees reported for Army training at Camp Gordon (now, Fort Gordon), Georgia.

Sources.

"Deserter Arrested in Macon County." *The Nashville, Tennessean and the Nashville American*, May 29, 1918, page 9.

"Last of Class One Sent from Macon." *The Nashville, Tennessean and the Nashville American*, May 29, 1918, page 9.

39. Hanes Busts up Stills

JOHNNIE Hanes was in his last year as Sheriff of Macon County and he went out of office by making several raids on distilleries in his jurisdiction. His first raid was near Red Boiling Springs where they found and destroyed a still.

About two weeks later, Hanes and eight deputies raided a distillery about one and one-half miles from Willette in Macon County's 7th District. The moonshiners hid the still far back in the woods and deep in a hollow. The nearest house to the still was a mile away. Hanes discovered that Mrs. Luelle Goad owned the property on which the still sat, but there was no evidence that she had any knowledge of the moonshine operation.

The Sheriff located the distillery around midnight on July 19, 1918. The moonshiners were not present, but Hanes and his deputies found 2,000 gallons of beer, some of it distilled and some of it ready to distill, several tubs, a furnace, and other items.

The Sheriff wanted to catch the whiskey makers badly and he waited on the scene until July 22 for them to return. Unable to wait any longer, the Sheriff ordered the distillery destroyed and he and his deputies returned to Lafayette.

Hanes related that there were many other wildcat whiskey distilleries remaining in Macon County. The Sheriff promised that before he left office he would to flush out as many moonshiners and to destroy as many stills as possible.

Sources.

Blankenship, Harold G. *History of Macon County, Tennessee.* Tompkinsville, Kentucky: Monroe County Press, 1986, page 155.

Gammon, CL. *Revenue Raiders: Macon County's Whiskey War.* Lafayette, Tennessee: Deep Read Press, 2022, page 81.

"Large Wildcat Still Is Captured." *Nashville Tennessean and The Nashville American*, July 21, 1918, page A5.

40. The Macon County Dog Tax

WILD and stray dogs were a big problem in rural America well into the 20th Century. Macon County was no exception. In June 1919, there were an estimated 13,330 dogs inside the Macon County border, many of them stray or wild. There was a real threat to cattle, fowl, sheep, and other livestock from these feral dogs. There was also a threat that wild dogs would spread diseases such as rabies to livestock and humans.

Before they could effectively deal with the stray dog problem, county officials had to determine which dogs had owners and which didn't. The County Court passed an ordinance requiring county citizens to pay a small tax on the dogs they owned. The authorities would consider all unclaimed dogs as strays or wild. County leaders planned to round up the strays and wild dogs, and if need be, destroy them.

In the middle of June 1919, Macon County Tax Assessor, W. W. Smith reported that the amount paid in dog taxes only amounted to $1,500, but he expected the amount to grow to $4,000 by the end of the tax year. Even at the larger amount, it would mean that thousands of dogs roamed the county without owners.

Macon County Trustee Connie Jent stated that to his knowledge, there had been no recent claims of wild dogs killing sheep within the county borders. Yet, a Nashville newspaper predicted that unless many more people than were expected to pay the dog tax did so, officials would initiate a "wholesale slaughter" of strays in Macon County.

Sources.

Blankenship, Harold G. *History of Macon County, Tennessee*. Tompkinsville, Kentucky: Monroe County Press, 1986, pages 157-158.

"Taxes Paid on Small Per Cent of Macon Dogs." *Nashville Tennessean and The Nashville American*, June 19, 1919, page 7.

41. Deputy Kills Prisoner

AGAIN, despite what some may think, wearing a badge does not give one free reign to break the law. A Macon County Deputy Sheriff found that out after a horrible incident in 1919.

On the morning July 12, 1919, near Red Boiling Springs, Macon County Deputy Sheriff Sam Hance served 20-year-old Homer Davis with an arrest warrant for the rather minor offense of public drunkenness.

Soon after Hance arrested him, Davis broke away from the deputy and tried to run into the nearby woods. As Davis ran, Hance drew his pistol quickly and fired one shot at the escaping man. The bullet struck Davis in the back, pierced his kidneys, and lodged near his spine. Friends summoned medical care for Davis, but he died soon after the shooting.

The killing outraged a good many citizens of Macon County and they demanded Hance's prosecution. Attending physician H. C. Hesson even listed the cause of death as homicide. A Grand Jury agreed with the doctor and it indicted the deputy for the murder.

The criminal court first scheduled to open on July 21, 1919 had Hance's case on the docket. However, the court allowed the postponement of the trial several times.

Hance finally went on trial in November 1919 charged with voluntarily manslaughter. The deputy could not deny that he had shot

Davis in the back and killed him. However, he contended that the killing was accidental.

Hance claimed that he fired a warning shot into the ground, but the bullet ricocheted, flew about 35 feet, and hit Davis in the back. Contrary to Hance's testimony, witnesses to the shooting testified that the Deputy took careful aim before firing directly at the fleeing Davis.

Another problem for Hance was that he and Davis had a contentious history with one another. For one thing, Hance had secured an indictment against Davis in November 1918, but nothing came of it.

In 1919, Hance applied for an appointment as Deputy Sheriff of Macon County. Sheriff Edwin O. "Ed" Sanders agreed to hire Hance, but required that the new deputy move from Clay County to Macon County. While Hance was preparing for his move, his house burned. Hance felt that Davis had burned the house down and swore out a warrant against his enemy charging him with arson. There was no evidence connecting Davis to the burning and Hance dropped the matter.

Then, in July 1919, Hance secured an invalid warrant that was more than a year old and set out to arrest Davis. This led directly to the shooting.

At 3 o'clock on the afternoon of November 21, the trial jury returned with a guilty verdict and Hance received a sentence of 2-5 years in prison.

Hance requested a new trial, which the judge denied. Hance then appealed to the Tennessee State Supreme Court.

On February 5, 1921, the Supreme Court heard Hance's appeal. Hance presented nothing during the hearing worthy of overturning verdict. The High Court rejected the appeal and ordered Hance to the state penitentiary to serve his term.

Sources.

Blankenship, Harold G. *History of Macon County, Tennessee.* Tompkinsville, Kentucky: Monroe County Press, 1986, page 137, 155.

Davis, Homer. *Tennessee Death Records, 1908-1965.* Nashville, Tennessee: Tennessee State Library and Archives.

"Day's Rulings of State's High Court." *Nashville Tennessean*, February 6, 1921, page 6.

Gammon, CL. *Revenue Raiders: Macon County's Whiskey War.* Lafayette, Tennessee: Deep Read Press, 2022, pages 95-97.

Officer Fatally Shoots Prisoner in Macon County." *Nashville Tennessean and The Nashville American*, July 13, 1919, page 7.

"S. H. Hance Given Prison Sentence." *Nashville Tennessean and The Nashville American*, November 23, 1919, page 5.

"Two Weeks of Court Open in Macon County." *Nashville Tennessean and The Nashville American*, July 21, 1919, page 5.

42. Trusting Sheriff Tricked

It is important for those working in law enforcement to develop a degree of trust with those they serve. Those behind the badge must have trust in their constituents too. At the same time, they should remember that many of those they deal with are criminals. If the law enforcers place their trust in the wrong people, they can have problems.

Many citizens of Macon County knew G. W. Harwood well. He had lived in Macon County for several years before moving to Nashville. At some point, a Chancery Court judge ordered Harwood to pay a judgment of $200. Harwood never paid the judgment and he never planned to pay it.

In the middle of July 1919, Macon County Sheriff Ed Sanders got word that Harwood was in Lafayette. The Sheriff located Sanders, presented him with the order of the Chancery Court, and took possession of the big, fancy Oldsmobile Harwood was driving.

Harwood said the trouble was the result of a big misunderstanding. He told the Sheriff that the car was not his, but that it belonged to a man in Nashville. When Sanders refused to return the car to Harwood, Harwood asked the Sheriff to drive him to Red Boiling Springs so he could solve the problem to everyone's satisfaction.

After a little thought, Sheriff Sanders agreed to drive Harwood to Red Boiling Springs in the confiscated Oldsmobile. When they arrived in Red Boiling Springs, the Sheriff stopped the car and got out to get a "cold drink." The trusting Sheriff left Harwood in the Oldsmobile unattended.

Harwood, who wasn't handcuffed, seized his opportunity. Before the Sheriff came back to the Oldsmobile, Harwood slid behind the wheel and sped away in it.

Stranded and red-faced, the Sheriff had to hire a man to drive him back to his office in Lafayette. Although he was embarrassed, Sheriff Sanders maintained a positive attitude. He predicted that Harwood would return to Lafayette, "sometime."

Sources.

Blankenship, Harold G. *History of Macon County, Tennessee.* Tompkinsville, Kentucky: Monroe County Press, 1986, page 155.

"Big Oldsmobile Converted Into 'Dodge' Quickly." *Nashville Tennessean and The Nashville American*, July 16, 1919, page 7.

43. A Dedicated Revenue Agent

DURING the time of National Prohibition, the United States government was serious about stamping out moonshine production in rural America. Since Macon County was a major producer of illegal alcohol, it was a fertile ground for Prohibition agents to work.

Elsie Jenkins hailed from the Red Boiling Springs/Pleasant Shade area. He received a commission as a Federal Prohibition Agent in 1921 and he wanted to make an immediate splash. Jenkins made one of his first raids in September 1921 near the Gibbs Crossroads community. During the raid, Jenkins arrested J. O. and E. J. Johnson, captured 5 gallons of whiskey, and confiscated an automobile.

Jenkins transported the Johnsons before a United States Commissioner named Barnes for arraignment. The Commissioner bound the men over to Federal Court.

Agent Elsie Jenkins continued his raids with the aid of agent W. B. Stone. They had plenty of opportunities.

In early June 1922, the agents raided the home of J. L. Yokley at Red Boiling Springs. During their search, they found a one-half gallon jug of "white liquor" (that is, clear whiskey). Yokley denied that the liquor was his, but Jenkins and Stone arrested him anyway. Commissioner Barnes placed Yokley under a

$500 bond and bound him over for trial in Federal Court.

The agents then went to Donnie Clark's General Store at Drapers Crossroads. The agents searched the store, but found nothing incriminating. As they were leaving the store, they witnessed Edgar Clark, Donnie Clark's brother, running into the woods with something in his hand.

Jenkins and Stone chased Edgar Clark down and questioned him. The questioning led to the seizure a one-half gallon jug of whiskey hidden in a tree stump. Edgar Clark said the whiskey belonged to his brother.

Armed with the liquor and Edgar Clark's statement, Jenkins and Stone went back to Donnie Clark, who admitted it was his whiskey.

Jenkins and Stone hauled Donnie Clark before Commissioner Barnes too. Barnes placed Clark under a $500 bond and bound him over to Federal Court.

Prohibition Agent Elsie Jenkins was good at his job and he evidently enjoyed it. He continued his raids for several years. For instance, in March 1924, the energetic Jenkins, aided by Constables Tom Colter and Sam White raided a distillery six about miles north of Lafayette.

The three men found and destroyed a nice 18-gallon "outfit," 200 gallons of beer, and four "fermenters." Jenkins and his men did not surprise anyone on the scene and they made no arrests during the raid.

Sources.

"Berries Or Not, Jars are Useful." *Nashville Tennessean*, June 7, 1922, page 9.

Gammon, CL. *Revenue Raiders: Macon County's Whiskey War*. Lafayette, Tennessee: Deep Read Press, 2022, page 101-103.

"New Raider Arrests Two And Seizes Car." *Nashville Tennessean*, September 27, 1921, page 5.

"Raiders Do Effective Work Against 'Shiners." *The Nashville Tennessean*, March 11, 1924, page 1.

44. Sheriff Frye Gunned Down

LAW enforcement officers never make a "routine" arrest. If an officer lets his guard down for, even an instant, he can find himself involved in a deadly encounter. Such was the case in Macon County in September 1927.

Virgil Frye was in the middle of his first term as Macon County Sheriff. Sheriff Frye had the reputation of being a fearless peace officer, especially when it came to enforcing liquor laws.

On Saturday, September 24, 1927, the Sheriff conducted a raid alone near the Willette community. Frye parked his car just off the road near a corncrib on the property of a man named Fleming. When Frye entered the corncrib, the Sheriff found Fleming and Earl Goad inside drinking whiskey.

When the men saw the Sheriff, they tried to escape and one of them tried to toss away a bottle partially filled with liquor. Frye ordered the men to stop and they did. He then arrested them and recovered the whiskey. But what started as a minor affair soon turned into a life or death situation.

Following the arrest, the Sheriff made an error in judgment. Goad had parked his car just off the road near Fleming's house. The Sheriff granted Goad's request to walk over to his automobile alone. When Goad got to his car, he pulled a shotgun out of the backseat and pointed it at Sheriff Frye. Frye drew his pistol and ordered Goad to drop the shotgun and Goad refused.

The standoff did not continue very long. Within seconds, the two men opened fire upon each other. After a few shots, Goad ran behind the Sheriff's car, which was just a few feet behind his own, and hunkered down.

Then, Frye made another mistake. From the way Goad moved, the Sheriff thought he had wounded him. Because he believed Goad would now surrender, Frye stopped firing. The pause almost cost him the Sheriff his life.

The Sheriff had not wounded Goad and Goad did not intend to surrender. After taking up a position behind the Sheriff's car, Goad fired twice more. Shotgun pellets tore into Sheriff Frye's chest, puncturing one of his lungs. Frye dropped to the ground and Goad skedaddled into the safety offered by the thick woods nearby.

Fleming did not run away when Goad did. Instead, he remained and administered first aid to the badly wounded Sheriff as best he could. The Sheriff was very strong; he never passed out.

Frye received transport and admission to Nashville's Baptist Hospital. While the wounds were not fatal in themselves, the doctors feared that infection or inflammation of his damaged lung might kill Sheriff Frye.

The shooting ignited perhaps the biggest manhunt in the history of Macon County, but it got underway late. Four of Frye's deputies were at a camp meeting revival at a church in the

Cedar Bluff community and they were not located immediately. After the manhunt did get started, scores of law enforcement agents and private citizens from Macon and the adjoining counties fanned out in the woods looking for Goad, but he avoided them.

Frye's wife, Florence, was at home very ill. She had recently had an operation and the authorities felt it wise that they not tell her about the shooting until after her husband was out of danger. Poor Florence Frye never recovered. She died on October 20, 1927.

Sheriff Frye did recover. After spending several days in the hospital, he returned home to finish recuperating. By early November 1927, Frye was back on the job, and his top target for arrest was Earl Goad.

During the evening of November 3, 1927, Frye intercepted Earl Goad as the fugitive drove down the road near his home. Frye was not alone this time. Those assisting the Sheriff were Henry Meadors, A. H. Andrews, Tilford Gregory, J. F. Hancock, B. C. Andrews, and J. W. Leath.

Goad did not offer any resistance and the Sheriff took the fugitive and the man with him, B. B. Donoho, into custody. Donoho denied any knowledge of the shooting and the authorities released him. A Justice of the Peace jailed Goad and bound him over for trial. Goad later made bond.

After several postponements, Earl Goad finally went on trial in May 1929. A jury heard the evidence, convicted him, and sentenced him to serve one year in the state penitentiary.

About seven months after Goad went to prison, a movement began to free him. Surprisingly, the leader of the effort to release Goad was the victim of the shooting, Macon County Sheriff Virgil Frye. Frye stated that he believed that Goad was too intoxicated on the day of the shooting to understand what he was doing. Frye held that had he been sober, Goad would have never harmed anyone. The jury members, although they had voted for conviction, joined Sheriff Frye in requesting the Governor issue the pardon.

On November 12, 1929, Governor Henry Horton reviewed the pardon request and ordered Goad freed.

Sources.

Blankenship, Harold G. *History of Macon County, Tennessee.* Tompkinsville, Kentucky: Monroe County Press, 1986, page 155.

"Donoho Is Cleared In Macon Hearing." *The Nashville Tennessean* November 7, 1927, page 12.

"Horton Pardons Three." *The Nashville Tennessean* November 13, 1929, page 10.

"Scores Search For Gunman As Sheriff is Shot." *The Nashville Tennessean* September 25, 1927, pages 1, 5.

"Wounded Sheriff Recovers, Naps Escaped Gunman." *The Nashville Tennessean* November 4, 1927, pages 14.

45. Posse Pursues Thieves

WHEN we think of a posse, we generally think of Old West Marshals gathering up townsfolk and chasing after notorious outlaws. However, the posse remained an important law enforcement tool in Macon County, and elsewhere, well into the 20th Century.

In 1930, Sheriff Virgil Brooks led a posse in pursuit of three boys. Apparently, the three youths had broken into several homes just across the border from Macon County in County, Kentucky. They had also broken into the Akersville, Kentucky post office at about 2 a.m. on July 13, 1930. Their take from the post office robbery was $25 and an automatic pistol.

The young crooks broke into White's General Store in Allen County, Kentucky as well. The robbers took pistol ammunition and other goods from the store.

The citizens in the area were upset and they pressured officials in both Kentucky and Tennessee to act. Authorities surmised that the robbers hid their ill-gotten gains in caves in the area and felt that a search of those caves might recover the loot and catch the young outlaws.

Sheriffs Fred Evans of Tompkinsville, Kentucky and Virgil Brooks of Macon County put together a posse of some fifty men. They scoured a line of territory stretching some twenty miles along the Macon County and Monroe County, Kentucky borders. The posse did not locate any of the suspects or any of the loot.

The Sheriffs told the media that they knew the identities of the boys, but they refused to reveal their names because the thieves were minors.

Sources.

Blankenship, Harold G. *History of Macon County, Tennessee.* Tompkinsville, Kentucky: Monroe County Press, 1986, page 155.

"Posse from Two Counties Hunt Housebreakers." *The Nashville Tennessean,* July 21, 1930, page 3.

46. The Bloody Truck Mystery

THIS story concerns the mystery surrounding Marion Bilbry, a truck driver from Glasgow, Kentucky. Bilbry drove for the Davidson Brothers wholesale grocery company. On the morning of October 9, 1930, he departed Glasgow with a load of goods earmarked for several general stores in Tennessee. He made some deliveries, but he never returned with his truck. It was unlike Bilbry to be late in returning to the warehouse and the manager reported him missing.

On October 10, authorities found Bilbry's vehicle near Red Boiling Springs, Tennessee. The truck contained traces of blood and had a single bullet hole in it. A woman that lived near where the officers found the truck said that during the night of October 9, she had heard "loud talk," followed by three gunshots.

Macon County Sheriff Virgil Brooks began investigating the mystery and he soon learned of rumors that someone had warned Bilbry not to come to Red Boiling Springs again. The rumor mill also spun the story that because of the threat, Bilbry began carrying a gun for his personal protection.

Sheriff Brooks then located a twenty-two-year-old man from Lafayette named Thurston King. King told the Sheriff that three young men had given him details of how they robbed and wounded the truck driver. King accused 19-year-old Cordell Parkhurst, 22-year-old

Foble Parkhurst, and 20-year-old Ben Smith. All three suspects lived in Red Boiling Springs.

Based on what King told him, Sheriff Brooks took the three young men into custody early on the morning of October 12 and held them in connection with the disappearance. Then, the Sheriff continued his investigation.

Sheriff Brooks went to the location that King told him the three said they had taken Bilbry for treatment after they had wounded him, but Bilbry was not there and Brooks could not establish that he ever had been there. Additionally, the frustrated Sheriff failed to find any evidence of Bilbry around the area where authorities had found the blood-streaked truck.

With no physical evidence, later on October 12, the Sheriff released his three suspects. He said that all three men denied any knowledge of Bilbry's disappearance and he could not hold them on suspicion alone regardless of his personal opinion. Sheriff Brooks added that he believed that someone murdered Bilbry, but had no proof of it.

Meanwhile, Bilbry's employers offered a $100 reward to anyone providing accurate information about the whereabouts of their driver. Davidson Brothers officials thought someone might have robbed Bilbry of about $50 he collected from merchants along his route the day he disappeared. Then, the robbers, according to the beliefs of the company officials, killed the driver and disposed of his body. Yet, it was all speculation and there was not enough evidence to continue the investigation.

Source.

"Youths Deny Part In 'Bloody Truck' Mystery." *The Nashville Tennessean,* October 13, 1930, page 3.

47. Man Kills In-Law

SADLY, disputes among in-laws are all too common. Sometimes those disputes lead to violence, and even death. The following account comes from the early springtime days of 1931.

Successful farmer, 69-year-old Josh White and his son-in-law, 32 year-old Taft Freeman had several arguments over time. White had ordered Freeman never to darken his door again. Freeman was not afraid of White. On the contrary, he desired an altercation with the feeble old man.

On March 31, 1931, Freeman, who was married to White's daughter, Rosie, got very drunk and decided to have it out with his father-in-law. Freeman came to the White farm with a wagonload of furniture. Freeman, who had a razor in his hand, walked up to White's front door, and tried to force his way into the house. When he could not get the door open, Freeman broke the door's window.

Fearful for his life, White raised his double-barreled 12-gauge shotgun, pulled the triggers, and hot lead flew from both barrels. The projectiles from one barrel wounded a mule standing on White's front lawn. The blast from the other barrel struck Freeman in the chest with pellets penetrating his heart and killing him instantly.

Sheriff Virgil Brooks investigated, declared the shooting an act of self-defense, and refused to file charges against the prosperous farmer. Coroner J. F. Hancock visited the scene of the shooting, agreed with the Sheriff Brooks, and decided there was no need to hold an inquest.

Source.

"Macon Countian Slain By His Father-In-Law." *The Nashville Tennessean,* March 13, 1931, page 10.

48. Speeder Disrupts Egg Hunt

EASTER remains an important holiday in Tennessee, as it does for much of America and the entire Christian world. Easter weekend traditionally marks the beginning of springtime in America and outside activities are a big part of it. These activities often include children searching for brightly colored eggs filled with candy or other prizes.

For many years, the annual Easter egg hunt at Hartsville, Tennessee was a major event. People from around middle Tennessee and southern Kentucky brought their children to Hartsville for a day of fun. However, in 1931, the Easter egg hunt almost turned tragic.

About 1,500 people flocked to Hartsville on the warm and sunny Saturday afternoon of April 4, 1931 for the annual egg hunt. There were smiles and laughter galore among the participants. Then suddenly, the happiness turned to horror.

Macon County resident, Ottis Gann, drove his car recklessly through the throng of people at a high rate of speed. After passing through the startled crowd, Gann sped on without checking to see if he had struck anyone.

Tennessee State Troopers Wayne Hargis and J. H. Duncan gave pursuit and followed Gann for several miles in a wild chase until they finally caught up with him and took him into custody.

The Troopers charged Gann with reckless driving and then they turned him over to the Trousdale County Sheriff. Additionally, the Sheriff charged Gann with transporting and possessing intoxicating liquor, and driving while drunk.

The good news was that Gann did not hurt or kill anyone and the festivities continued despite the frightening disturbance.

Sources.

Gammon, CL. *Revenue Raiders: Macon County's Whiskey War*. Lafayette, Tennessee: Deep Read Press, 2022, pages 101-102.

"Three Arrested By State Patrolmen." *The Nashville Tennessean,* April 6, 1931, page 2. Courtesy of the Tennessee Electronic Library.

49. Young Bank Robbers

JESSE James and his gang staged the first daytime bank robbery in the United States on February 13, 1866. Bank robberies continued sporadically until the late 1920s, when they increased dramatically. For the next decade or so, banks were a favorite target of criminals. Perhaps the notoriety gained by successful bank robberies influenced a couple of youths to attempt to try it themselves.

On Friday, July 24, 1931, two young men wearing black facemasks drove up in front of the Bank of Hermitage Springs, in Clay County, Tennessee. The men had the intention of robbing the bank and driving away with a big haul.

After the driver parked the car, the other would be robber climbed out, went into the bank, and walked up to the teller's cage.

The thief said to cashier Weldon Meadows, "Stick 'em up. I'm holding up your bank."

The cashier responded to the ridiculous looking man, "No. You're joking."

Taken aback a little, the robber retorted, "Joking? I've got a gun. Stick 'em up."

Meadows continued to refuse to comply. He recognized the person in front of him, "What a joker you are," Meadows spoke with a chuckle. "I know you even if your face is blackened and all plastered up."

The robber was fast losing his confidence. He repeated nervously, "Stick 'em up."

Sensing the robber's fearful indecisiveness, Meadows took the opportunity to duck behind the teller's cage and call out loudly, "The bank's being robbed! Help! Bank's being robbed!"

Frightened and confused, the robber ran out of the bank, jumped into the car, and his partner began to drive them away.

I. R. Browning was on the street outside the bank when he heard Meadows yelling. As the robber car started to leave, Browning drew his gun and opened fire. He didn't hit the suspects, but he did cause the driver to speed away toward Red Boiling Springs as quickly as the old car would carry the outlaws.

One of Browning's bullets may have pierced a gas or oil line on the getaway car. Whatever the reason, the vehicle's motor caught fire about two miles west of the bank. The failed bank robbers abandoned the blazing vehicle and scampered into the wooded hills to avoid their pursers.

Clay County Sheriff Denton Alexander "Alex" Spear gathered his bloodhounds and made out after the fleeing felons on foot. Spear was certain that if the criminals' feet "don't last forever," his bloodhounds would catch their prey.

The bloodhounds picked up the scent of the robbers and followed the trail for several hours, even after nightfall. Besides Sheriff Spear and his hounds, townsfolk also followed along in pursuit of the robbers.

Despite his confidence in his dogs, Sheriff did not apprehend the bank robbers before they crossed over the state line into Kentucky. Yet, entering the Kentucky Commonwealth did not afford the fleeing men their freedom. Based on what Weldon Meadows told him, Sheriff Spear was certain that he knew the identity of one of the robbers. Spear passed the information along to Kentucky authorities and during the afternoon of July 25, Scottsville, Kentucky chief of police Proctor Morgan took the two exhausted young men into custody and held them for "suspicion."

The young men identified themselves as 18-year-old Seth Carver and 20-year-old Vestal King. Both men were from of Macon County.

Chief Morgan transferred the failed outlaws to the custody to the Macon County Sheriff's Department and Clay County Sheriff Alex Spear then went to Lafayette, picked up the pair and drove them to Celina where he lodged them in the Clay County jail.

Under questioning, Vestal King, seeing no way out of his predicament, confessed to trying to rob the bank. He further conceded that Seth Carver was his accomplice. Carver refused to admit that he was a part of the hold up attempt.

Even though the wannabe bank robbers came away from their adventure with nothing but a destroyed vehicle, they still had a preliminary hearing on July 27 to answer for their crime. During the hearing, King again admitted his part in the farcical hold up, but Carver refused to make any kind of a statement.

If nothing else, after it was all settled, the youths could brag that they were ahead of other, more famous bank robbers like John Dillinger and Bonnie and Clyde. Those infamous outlaws didn't hit their first banks King and Carver had tried it. King and Carver could also be happy that they didn't die in a hailstorm of bullets, as did Dillinger, Bonnie and Clyde and so many other notorious bank robbers.

Sources.

"Cashier's Yell Puts Intended Bandits to Flight Near Celina." *The Nashville Tennessean,* July 26, 1931, pages 1-2.

Gorn, Elliott J. Dillinger's Wild Ride: *The Year That Made America's Public Enemy Number One.* London: Oxford University Press, 2011, page 101.

No Author Credited. *History of Clay and Platte Counties, Missouri.* St. Louis: National Historical Company, 1885, pages 259-260.

"One of Pair, Held at Celina, Admits Trying to Rob Bank." *The Nashville Tennessean,* July 27, 1931, page 10.

Ramsey, Winston G. (editor). *On the Trail of Bonnie and Clyde: Then and Now.* London: After the Battle Books, 2003, pages 118, 122.

"Youth Admits Part In Attempted Bank Holdup." *The Nashville Tennessean,* July 28, 1931, page 1.

50. Jackson County Raid

CATCHING moonshiners was something of an art form. It required a degree of stealth and cunning. It also required courage. Raiders relied on informants to provide them with accurate information as to the whereabouts of stills. If the information was incorrect, the raiders might walk into an ambush. Thankfully, the agents in the following story had accurate information.

During the early morning hours of August 23, 1931, law enforcement officers were on the prowl. Deputy Sheriffs Ernest Ramsey and Will Smith, along with Constables Hubert Tuck and James Sutton slipped across the line from Macon into Jackson County, Tennessee. There they raided a moonshine operation on Hudson Creek.

The officers arrested Dewey Hudson, Gene Holliers, and Malcolm Massey, all of Macon County. The arresting officers also found "one of the most complete wildcat stills ever operated in this section." The still was a beauty. It was copper and it had a capacity of 110 gallons. Along with the still, the officers confiscated 600 gallons of beer.

The Macon County officials turned the moonshiners over to Jackson County Deputy Sheriff, Harley Webb, who took them to the jail in Gainesboro. The suspects went before Justice of the Peace, W. S. Hance and Hance bound them over to the November term of the Jackson County criminal court.

Source.

"Three Caught in Raid." *The Nashville Tennessean,* August 26, 1931, page 8. Courtesy of the Tennessee Electronic Library.

51. A Clever Counterfeiter

SADLY, all too often, some of the most talented individuals among us choose to use their gifts for unproductive, or even criminal, pursuits. This is the story of a talented man who chose to misuse his gifts.

Chester Jones of the Green Valley community was one that chose to go down the wrong path – at least for a while. Jones, a 39-year-old watchmaker from Macon County, developed a plan to make some quick cash by counterfeiting currency. On February 4, 1932, Jones saw his scheme fall apart when Federal Secret Service Agent Albert Vaughn and Macon County Sheriff Virgil Brooks came to his house and arrested him. Jones confessed to his crimes quickly.

Most counterfeiters create phony paper money, not so Chester Jones. He molded fake coins. Jones informed Agent Vaughn and Sheriff Brooks of the location of three sets of molds he had constructed.

Sheriff Virgil Brooks placed Jones in the county jail and then went to a tree stump the suspect had mentioned and found the very well constructed "Babbitt metal" molds. Babbitt metal is a soft alloy sometimes called "white metal." It is ideal for the use Jones made of it.

Jones used a genuine $5 gold piece as his model. He pressed the gold piece into each of the hot, malleable metal molds making a very good likeness of the coin in them. When the molds cooled and became hard, he poured molten lead or another base metal into them making excellent likenesses of the gold coin. When they hardened, he removed the fake coins from the molds and then dipped them into melted gold producing replicas that were difficult to tell from real thing.

Jones claimed that he had only produced a few of his counterfeit coins before his arrest. However, since he made three molds, it is likely that he intended to produce a large quantity of fake gold pieces.

The counterfeiting charge was a federal offense. On Saturday, February 6, 1932, Jones appeared at a preliminary hearing before a Federal Magistrate. The Magistrate set bond for Jones at $1,000. Jones made his bond on February 9 and went home with his family.

During his confession, Jones implicated his partner in crime, Ernest King. King was a 20-year-old man that lived in the Jones household. King's job was to pass the counterfeits Jones manufactured. Shortly after Jones accused him, authorities in Bowling Green, Kentucky arrested King and charged him with peddling the fake gold pieces. For whatever reason, the Magistrate set King's bond at $3,000. The young man had trouble making his bond and evidently, Jones refused to help him get out of jail.

Possession of gold was a hot topic for debate in the early 1930s. On April 5, 1933, President Roosevelt issued an Executive Order making it illegal to "horde" gold. Then, on January 30,

1934, the Gold Reserve Act took effect and Americans could no longer hold gold with the exception of jewelry and collectors' coins. The ban on gold remained in effect until December 31, 1974.

Sources.

"Gold Reserve Act." *Statutes at Large of the United States of America from March 1933 to June 1934.* Washington: Government Printing Office, 1934, pages 337–344.

Hellemans, Alexander and Bryan Bunch. *The Timetables of Science.* New York: Simon & Schuster, 1988, page 305.

"Hoarders Face Heavy Penalty Under U. S. Writ." *Chattanooga Daily Times.* April 6, 1933. page 1.

Public Law 93-373: "An Act to provide for increased participation by the United States in the International Development Association and to permit United States citizens to purchase, hold, sell, or otherwise deal with gold in the United States or abroad."

Scott, Betty C. Meadows, *Macon County, Tennessee Obituaries and Articles Volume 1.* Lafayette, Tennessee: Ridge Runner Publications and Genealogy Research, 2003, page 15.

"Two Held in Gold Counterfeit Case." *The Nashville Tennessean*, February 5, 1932, page 16.

52. Driving Legally

No one enjoys paying taxes, but most understand that certain government services are necessary and that taxes pay for them. Purchasing license plates and tags help provide some of those necessary services. This chapter looks at some things involved with purchasing license plates and tags in Macon County during the 1930s.

Get Tags or Face Arrest

During the Great Depression, it was difficult for many Macon County residents to scrape together enough cash to pay for much of anything. Even coming up with the necessary funds to purchase license plates for their vehicles was difficult.

Macon County Sheriff Virgil Brooks understood the situation faced by many citizens and he felt compassion for motorists. However, he also had to enforce the law. The Sheriff put out the word that because of the Great Depression he would give drivers until February 8, 1932 to purchase their new "license numbers." However, he warned that after that date he would arrest anyone driving illegally.

Brooks also reminded drivers that all vehicles had to have two working headlights and two working taillights. The Sheriff stated that he would arrest any person driving vehicles without proper lighting.

Get New Tags Immediately

In February 1935, the state of Tennessee mandated that all motorists purchase new license tags immediately or be subject to arrest. However, the Sheriff of Macon County promised not to arrest anyone on their way to the courthouse to purchase new tags.

In 1935, the price of tags for lighter cars such as "Chevrolet, Ford, Plymouth, Essex, and Pontiac" was $7.85. Owners with vehicles weighing 3,500 pounds or more paid a $10.35 fee for their plates.

A New Plate Design

1936 Tennessee License Plate

The Tennessee government did things in the mid 1930s to entice more citizens to drive. On August 29, 1935, J. C. Baxter of the Motor Vehicle Division of the State Department of Finance and Taxation announced that the 1936 Tennessee's license plates shape would be in the outline of the state map. Baxter related that Tennessee plates were the only ones in the country fashioned in the outline of a state. Baxter also predicted sales of Tennessee license plates in 1936 to surpass previous records by as much as 50,000.

Pennies for License Plates

During the 1930s, money was always scarce. Many households had to save every penny – literally. Oakley and Alice Cook of the Fairview community were among the penny pinchers. In early 1936, the husband and wife began putting every loose penny in a large glass jar, saving them for something important. Naturally, keeping their car licensed legally was important and the couple decided to use their saved coppers for that purpose.

On April 3, 1937, the Cooks brought their jar filled with pennies to the office of County Court Clerk Fred D. Gregory and said they wanted to use them to purchase new license plates. Their method of payment surprised Gregory, but he counted out the 785 pennies needed and issued the Cooks license plates bearing the number C 185-743.

As it turned out, the Cooks brought 28 more pennies with them than they needed. This gave them a good start for the next time they needed license plates.

Sources.

Public domain image of a license plate from 1936.

Scott, Betty C. Meadows, *Macon County, Tennessee Obituaries and Articles Volume 1.* Lafayette, Tennessee: Ridge Runner Publications and Genealogy Research, 2003, pages 13, 89, 107

Scott, Betty C. Meadows, *Macon County, Tennessee Obituaries and Articles Volume 2.* Lafayette, Tennessee: Ridge Runner Publications and Genealogy Research, 2003, page 20.

53. The Willie Holland Murder

WITH the possible exception of serial killings, all intentional homicides have motives. But sometimes it is very difficult to ascertain the exact motivation of a given murderer. When the authorities can find no concrete motive for a slaying, and there is no eyewitness to the murder, a conviction becomes an almost impossible task.

About 8 o'clock on the early springtime evening of March 31, 1932, 25-year-old William A. "Willie" Holland appeared at the home of James Willis in the Gap of the Ridge community. Holland, who was 25, was riding a mule. He said he did not know his way home and Willis gave him directions. During the conversation, Holland said the "Sanders boys" had mistreated him, but he did not identify anyone specifically or relate how they wronged him.

Shortly after Holland rode toward home on his mule, Willis heard the sound of a gate rattle followed by a shot ringing out. Holland swore at the unknown shooter and shouted, "Shoot again!" Then Willis heard the report of a second shot, followed Holland by crying out from the pain of the pistol wound he suffered.

Fearing the worst, Willis started toward the sound of the gunfire and came upon a neighbor named Jodie Sanders. Sanders told Willis there had been a shooting. The two men continued until they found the badly wounded Willie

Holland near the gate leading into the Sanders property. Holland was under a tree lying on his left side.

Willis left Sanders with Holland while he went for help. When Willis returned, Sanders was gone and Holland was no longer under the tree. Willis eventually found Holland behind a barn about fifty yards away from his original location.

Friends took Holland to Whittemore & Doss's store where Dr. I. L. Roark attended the wounded man. Roark found that the bullet, fired from a pistol, entered the young man just below his right ribcage, penetrated his intestines, and remained in his body.

Lafayette didn't have adequate medical facilities to treat Holland successfully and his family took him home and later rushed him to the hospital at Scottsville, Kentucky. There, Dr. Lattie Graves of Scottsville and Dr. G. Y. Graves of Bowling Green, Kentucky operated on the young man, but they could not save him. Holland died at about 5 o'clock on the morning of April 1.

Believing that he knew the identities of the murderers, the victim's father, Granville T. Holland, swore out warrants for Jodie Sanders and Jodie's three sons, Buster, George, and Raymond. The four accused men denied any knowledge of the killing.

On April 5, the Sanders men appeared before Justice of the Peace, Ray Holland for a preliminary hearing. The largest crowd at the Macon County Courthouse in years attended the hearing and six attorneys took part in the proceedings.

There was no eyewitness to the shooting, except the deceased victim, and the Justice Holland ruled the young man's statements to Willis were incompetent as "death bed testimony" because he did not believe he was dying when he made his remarks. Besides that, the prosecution could not discern any clear motive for the killing.

After questioning Dr. Roark, Granville Holland, Ethel Sanders, and James Willis, the prosecutors, despite what they may have believed, admitted that they lacked the evidence necessary to pursue an indictment and dropped all charges against the Sanders men.

Sources.

Scott, Betty C. Meadows, *Macon County, Tennessee Obituaries and Articles Volume 1*. Lafayette, Tennessee: Ridge Runner Publications and Genealogy Research, 2003, page 17.

"Seek Bridegroom Killer." *The Nashville Tennessean*, April 2, 1932, page 1.

54. The Stolen Smokes Shooting

PEOPLE make stupid decisions when they are drunk. While often these stupid decisions lead to humorous results, sometimes they lead to tragedy.

On Sunday afternoon, April 2, 1932 a stupid decision by a drunken man almost caused the death of two boys.

Wint Johnson was a married man with children. He lived in the Walnut Shade community. Johnson was drinking heavily as he tooled around eastern Macon County in his car on that Sunday afternoon.

Johnson stopped and gave a ride to William "Bill" Donoho and Doyle Hudson. He then drove them to the home of Bedford Newberry who lived near the Willette community. The three got out of Johnson's car, but an incident happened before they went inside Newberry's house.

Naturally, the drunken Johnson was not thinking clearly. At some point, he became angry and accused Hudson of stealing his pack of cigarettes. Taken aback, Hudson denied that he had taken the smokes. Suddenly, Johnson pulled his .25-caliber automatic pistol from his pocket, held it near Hudson's face, and pulled the trigger several times. Luckily, the weapon, which was probably empty, would not fire.

Johnson, still intent on murder, ran into Newberry's house, grabbed a shotgun, and came back outside. Understanding their lives were in peril, Donoho and Hudson turned and ran, but before they were out of range, Johnson fired the shotgun.

Pellets struck Donoho in the back and Hudson in the heel. Luckily, neither of the victims suffered serious wounds.

Officer Hubert Knight came to the scene, arrested Johnson, took him to Lafayette, and deposited him in the Macon County jail. Johnson faced charges of drunk driving, possessing liquor, carrying a weapon, and assault with intent to commit murder in the first-degree.

Sources.

Gammon, CL. *Revenue Raiders: Macon County's Whiskey War*. Lafayette, Tennessee: Deep Read Press, 2022, pages 103-104.

Scott, Betty C. Meadows. *Macon County, Tennessee Obituaries and Articles Volume 1*. Lafayette, Tennessee: Ridge Runner Publications and Genealogy Research, 2003, page 54.

55. Bloodhounds at Webbtown

WE have all seen movies and television dramas about prison guards, usually evil southerners, using bloodhounds to chase escapees (wrongly convicted, of course) through forests and swamps of mythical locales. More times than not, the convicts avoid the bloodhounds and remain free until they can prove their innocence.

Evidently, Tennessee bloodhounds were superior to the Hollywood variety. Tennessee prisons employed bloodhounds with great effect. Beyond that, county officials often hired owners of well-trained bloodhounds to track down fugitives that local law enforcement agents could not find. The bloodhounds usually did an excellent job of locating fugitives quickly.

On June 11, 1932, there was a break-in at the Leath & Ward General Store in Macon County's Webbtown community. Local officials sought out J. E. Sullivan of Celina to help them. Sullivan had some of the best bloodhounds in Tennessee and he agreed to put his fine animals on the trail of the culprits.

The persistent hounds put their noses to the ground, picked up a scent, barked in their low, guttural tones, and followed the trail for about eight miles.

The dogs stayed on the trail and they eventually caught up with the alleged robbers.

Authorities captured suspects Walter Hargis and Lloyd Swindle, both of Webbtown.

Hargis confessed to the crime. He returned most of the $25 he had taken and all the goods he and his alleged confederate pilfered from the store. Then, Sheriff Virgil Brooks lodged Hargis in the Macon County Jail.

Source.

"Catch Alleged Robbers." *The Nashville Tennessean*, June 14, 1932, page 10.

56. The Courthouse Arson Case

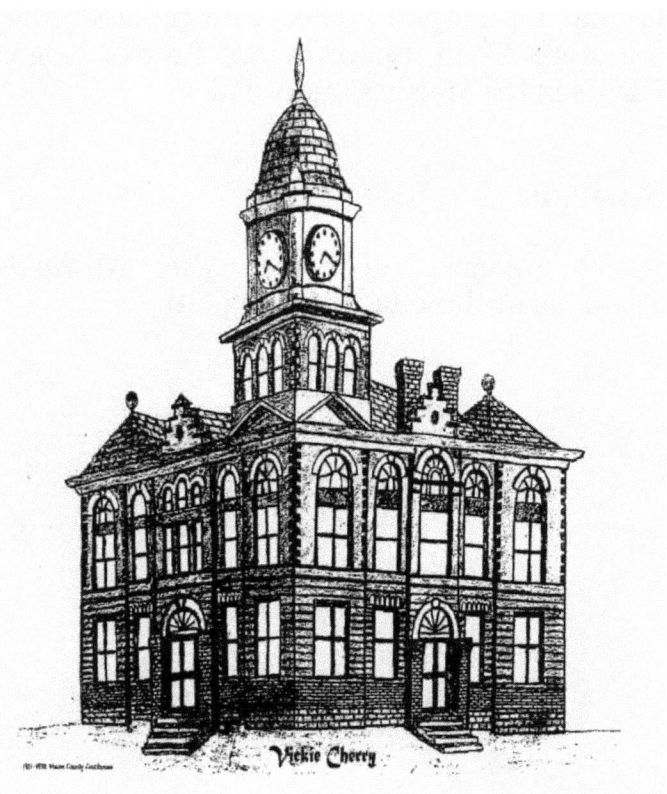

Illustration of Old Courthouse by Vickie Cherry, used with permission

FOR more than a century, courthouse fires were commonplace in Tennessee. Between 1830 and 1930, more than 50 courthouses in the Volunteer State caught fire. Since virtually all those courthouses were wooden structures, most of them suffered complete destruction.

Beyond the buildings themselves, irreplaceable records were also lost.

Macon County lost three courthouses to fire. The first burned in 1860 and the second went up in blazes in 1901.

The county's courthouse built after the 1901 fire, was a beauty. It was 50 feet by 50 feet and stood two stories tall. It had a cupola with a large clock face inserted in it. County fathers never saw fit to spend the $400 necessary to install a working clock, but the clock face was still pretty to look at. There were large offices on all corners of both floors of the building. It had large courtroom on the second floor and a balcony capable of seating a number of people if the courtroom became overcrowded. Additionally, there was a beautiful spiral staircase leading from the ground floor to the courtroom and the balcony.

[Note: The *Macon County Times* issue of September 17, 1936 stated the old courthouse was 60 feet square.]

Monday, July 4, 1932 was a national holiday, and the citizens of Macon County always enjoy celebrating Independence Day. However, heavy rains that morning put a damper on some activities in Lafayette and elsewhere in the outlying county. Oddly, the chagrin-causing downpour proved to be a blessing in disguise.

Holiday or not, most locals turned in early on the evening of July 4. Farm families never had days off. Because of the labor involved, farm families needed as much rest as possible. They had to rise early, have a hearty breakfast, milk the cows, and do scores of chores before getting to the actual work in their fields or homes. Naturally, when the citizens of Lafayette settled in that evening, they did not expect what was about happen.

A good many citizens of Lafayette found themselves shaken from their slumber about 11 o'clock on the night of July 4. Bells were ringing, men fired shots into the air, and husky voices filled the summer night with the cries of, "FIRE! FIRE! FIRE!" Jumping to their feet, the aroused citizens learned the Macon County Courthouse was burning out of control.

At about 10:30 p.m., Lester Allen noticed the blaze that had started in the office of Macon County Trustee Washington C. "Wash" Patterson. Allen called for help and began to fight the blaze. Several minutes later, County Sheriff Virgil Brooks, Wilson Allen, H. W. Bandy, Joe West, and several others joined in the losing battle to control the fast growing flame. Some felt that had a few more men joined the battle they may have been able to prevent the fire from devouring the entire building. Others held that no number of firefighters could have made a difference.

Armed with nothing but handheld fire extinguishers, the brave men forced their way into the quickly deteriorating office of the Trustee. However, the wicked flames, smoke, and heat soon forced them from the office.

Their inability to stop the fire where it began convinced the men that the building was lost and they decided to save as many of county records as they could before the complete engulfment of the building. The effort to save records was somewhat successful. The firefighters were able to secure most of the documents housed in the offices of the Chancery Court Clerk, Circuit Court Clerk, County Court Clerk, and the Register of Deeds. Beyond that, they rescued most of the fixtures from those offices. School Superintendant D. Henry Piper collected most of the items from his second story office. County Attorneys, Smith and Holland, lost some papers and retrieved others. Virtually all the books in Trustee Patterson's office burned, but a number of paper checks and an amount of gold in his safe escaped destruction. However, the heat scorched the checks badly.

A large group of citizens rushed forward to help prevent the fire from spreading to the other wooden structures on the town square. Lafayette had no fire truck of its own, but authorities sent out calls to nearby Hartsville and Gallatin, Tennessee, and Scottsville, Kentucky for help. Only the fire engine from Hartsville appeared. It arrived at about midnight, too late to do much good.

While the efforts of all involved were heroic, it was pure luck that the town avoided losing most of the buildings on the Public Square in the conflagration. Lafayette was fortunate that the southerly wind was not strong enough to fan the flames very much and that the heavy rains from earlier in the day soaked the wooden buildings and helped keep the fire from spreading.

It was also a matter of good luck that no one suffered serious injury during the fire.

Throughout the day on July 5, hundreds of citizens from across Macon County made the pilgrimage to the town square to see the ruins of the tabernacle of local government. The courthouse that had once been described as "one of the best arranged in the Upper Cumberland" was now mostly a pile of smoldering ash, and a couple of burned out walls that had to be pulled down for safety's sake.

The bean counters got together and determined that the county only had enough insurance to cover about one-half of the estimated loss of $20,000.

Regardless of the fact that the courthouse was gone, the business of government had to continue and county offices had to reopen. Authorities decided to hold the session of the County Court scheduled to open on July 18 in the high school building. County Court Clerk Franklin Pierce "Frank" Dixon, and Circuit Court Clerk B. V. Chamberlain established temporary offices in the building previously occupied by the Farmers and Merchants Bank & Trust Co. Register C. H. Dillard reopened his office upstairs in the Citizens Bank Building. D. Henry Piper made his office in his home.

At some point, questions arose as to exactly how the fire of July 4, 1932 began. However, no official investigation began until V. D. Bohanan, the Chair of the Macon County Court, hired "special" attorneys from Nashville,

Wynne F. Clouse, and Harry H. Chitwood to look into it. The attorneys in turn, hired Nashville detectives, Ted Vaughn and Joe Williams and tasked them to investigate the fire.

In their four-week investigation, Vaughn and Williams found enough circumstantial evidence for authorities to go to a Grand Jury and obtain indictments against Trustee Wash Patterson and County Court Clerk Frank Dixon for arson. The Grand Jury also indicted Dixon on embezzlement charges.

According to a prosecutor in another case against Dixon, "an audit ... made during the year 1933 of the records and accounts of the County officials of Macon County ... disclosed a most unsavory condition of affairs, especially with respect to the accounts of F. P. Dixon, former County Court Clerk." The prosecutor continued that Dixon "resigned his office after ouster proceedings had been filed against him and he and his bondsmen have heretofore paid and agreed to pay to the County and State between eight thousand and nine thousand dollars on account of revenues collected by him [that are] unaccounted for . . ."

Patterson, on the other hand, did not resign. He always denied any wrongdoing strongly. He won reelection easily in 1932, but later, the state brought ouster proceedings against him. The charges the state made against Patterson included "intoxication, gambling, and other derelictions." Patterson denied the charges and demanded a jury trial. The jury acquitted him and the Tennessee Supreme Court upheld the acquittal.

Trustee Patterson remained in office until his term expired in 1934. Additionally, Patterson seemed to retain the respect of a large portion of the citizens even after the fire. On February 9, 1933, the *Macon County Times* reported that on the previous Monday, "Wash Patterson, County Trustee, was busy from morning to night taking care of taxpayers."

In 1934, Patterson entered the race for Macon County Sheriff against John "Jack" Creasey, but he dropped out before the election.

Not only were Patterson and Dixon county officials, they were also business partners. The two jointly owned the Hotel Lincoln in Red Boiling Springs, Tennessee.

Dixon was ill and in the hospital, which caused the postponement of the trial twice. Meanwhile Vaughn and Williams had not received payment for their services. On August 6, 1935, *The Nashville Tennessean* reported that after a "heated argument", the County Court deferred the claim of Vaughn and Williams until the Circuit Court disposed of the case against Patterson and Dixon.

The Patterson Arson Trial

On November 20, 1935, the Dixon/Patterson case came before the Circuit Court in Lafayette for a third time and a large crowd turned out to see it. Finis E. Harris, a judge from Cookeville, was sitting in for Judge Harry Camp. Camp could not preside because he was sick at home in Sparta.

The proceedings began with testimony from doctors from the Madison, Tennessee sanatorium where Dixon was staying. They told Judge Harris that Dixon was too ill to leave his hospital bed and stand trial. Judge Harris continued the Dixon case.

Interesting, even Dixon's health issues were cause for controversy. On March 5, 1934, the Mutual of Omaha insurance company filed suit in federal court seeking to cancel the $10,000 policy it issued Dixon in October 1932. Mutual of Omaha contended that Dixon concealed the fact that he was "suffering with various physical ailments" when he applied for the policy.

Wash Patterson didn't want another delay. He informed the judge he was ready for his trial and his case proceeded.

On the morning of November 20, 1935, the court selected a jury composed of Bratton Brawner, Lloyd Cothron, C. G. Doss, W. H. Ford, Yerby Gregory, Lee Hanes, Emerson Jones, W. B. Kirby, Willie Purcell, Jim Scott, Frank Swindle, and Herman Tuck.

As is required by law, the court heard the formal reading of the indictment. The state charged Patterson with (1) setting fire to and burning the Macon County courthouse, (2) causing the burning of the courthouse, (3) aiding and procuring the burning of the courthouse, and (4) conspiracy to burn the courthouse. After the reading of the indictment, Patterson entered a pled not guilty.

District Attorney General John Mitchell had a strong team in Lafayette to prosecute Patterson. Those assisting Mitchell included Assistant District Attorney General Baxter Key, as well as Clouse, and Chitwood.

Although he faced formidable opposition, Wash Patterson sat at the defense table alone. Patterson, who had never studied law, did not ascribe to the old adage that a person who defends himself has a fool for a client. He determined that he would manage his own case.

Prosecutors contended that the motivation for the arson was simple. They alleged that Dixon and Patterson were involved in a failing business enterprise and in order to get out of their predicament, they embezzled county funds. Then, when investigations threatened to expose them, the penniless politicians tried to destroy all record of their guilt by burning down the courthouse.

For his part, Patterson denied he had any motive to burn the courthouse because he had stolen no money.

V. D Bohanan testified first. He related the details of the fire, as he understood them. Under cross-examination, Bohanan conceded that the final report of the auditors found no shortage of funds under Patterson's care. However, the prosecution countered that since Patterson's books burned in the fire, if a shortage existed, the auditors would not have been able to discover it.

Merlin A. West testified that when he entered the Trustee's office he used a fire extinguisher to spray several large record books that were ablaze. He said he put the books out thrice, but each time, the flames flared up again. West testified that fire ignited behind the Trustee's office door as well. He continued that he believed that someone had doused the books and other items in the office with gasoline.

The state attempted to build on the idea that the arsonists had used gasoline or a similar accelerant in the Trustee's office. One of those that battled the blaze testified that there was a "peculiar" odor in the courthouse's "foggy, smoky" air.

With the preliminaries out of the way, the state was ready to bring out its star witness. The prosecution called Lassie Mae White. White's testimony was explosive. She was formerly from Lafayette, but she had moved to Nashville where she operated a beauty parlor. White said she spoke with both Patterson and Dixon in Nashville shortly before the fire and heard them say, "If that damn courthouse would burn down, we would be safe."

White continued that Patterson owed her money, and that he told her he was in "great trouble." White said that Patterson admitted to her that his financial worries had caused him to embezzle county funds for his personal use.

White told the court that she was in the courthouse on July 4 shortly before Lester Allen sounded the alarm that the building was on fire and that she heard Patterson tell an unidentified man "stay with it 'til it gets going good."

Patterson's cross-examination of White was contentious and personal. It soon degenerated into an argument in which a series of "accusations and insinuations were hurled back and forth."

The state attempted to bolster Lassie White's testimony by calling her son James to the stand. The 13-year-old boy confirmed that he and his mother were in the courthouse on the night of the fire and he supported most of his mother's other testimony as well. When James White left the stand, the prosecution rested its case.

Patterson began his defense by taking the stand in his own behalf. He hotly denied that he knew anything about the fire. Patterson admitted that he was having money woes, but he said that his problems did not lead him to commit any crimes. He also told the court that he could not possibly have torched the courthouse because he left the building "about sunset," on July 4, which was hours before the fire ignited.

Prosecutor Wynne Clouse cross-examined Patterson roughly. Clouse sought to establish a connection between the former Trustee and a number of underworld figures operating out of Nashville. Patterson denied most of the allegations flatly, but when asked about one Nashville gambler in particular, Patterson exercised his Fifth Amendment right to refuse to answer because it might tend to incriminate him.

After Patterson left the stand, the judge recessed the court for the day.

The second and final day of the trial took place on November 21. During closing arguments, General Attorney General Mitchell spoke to the jury for half an hour. Mitchell stated that the jury had three charges to resolve, (1) the charge against Patterson for burning the courthouse, (2) the charge that Patterson conspired to burn the courthouse, and (3) the charge that Patterson caused the burning of the courthouse through other agents. If Patterson was guilty of any of those charges, he was guilty of arson.

Wynne Clouse then went over the testimony of the prosecution witnesses again.

For his part, Patterson closed by roaring at the jury with passion that he was innocent. He lashed out at Bohanan and others he considered his enemies, "If the County Court and the County Judge had not hounded me for the past three years, I would have had plenty of food, and clothing for my family, whereas, today I haven't any."

Patterson reiterated that he left his office on the evening of the fire at about 7 o'clock and went home where he had dinner. Then, he visited William W. "Bill" Blankenship and tried to borrow some money from him.

Bill Blankenship was one of the most respected men in the community. He had served as Sheriff of Macon County from 1898 to 1902 and again from 1920 to 1926. Unfortunately, he could not verify Patterson's story. Blankenship had died on February 27, 1935.

Patterson said he could not secure a loan from Bill Blankenship. Then he continued, "I went to Red Boiling Springs to see Mrs. B. W. Chitwood."

After Chitwood turned down Patterson's request for funds, he visited Mrs. Louise Warner's apartment. Warner also declined to loan Patterson any money.

Patterson told the jury that after he left Warner's hotel room, he went bowling. He said he was still bowling when he learned of the fire at the courthouse.

Then, Patterson tore into Lassie White. He branded her a perjurer. He denied that he had ever owed her any money. He also impugned her character.

Patterson, tears filling his eyes, ended by saying that he had no connection to the fire whatever. He claimed that he was the victim of a conspiracy and he pleaded with the jury to acquit him.

It was clear that Patterson had touched many of those in the courtroom. Not only were some of the spectators weeping, several of the jurors were fighting back tears as well.

The jurors left the courtroom to begin their deliberations at 3:55 p.m., and it was no surprise when a mere 80 minutes after they went out, they were back with a verdict. At 5:15 p.m., the jury pronounced Patterson not guilty of all the charges against him.

Patterson felt unharmed in the eyes of the community by the accusations and court trial. He even attempted to return to elective office in 1938. Patterson had formerly served as Chairman of the Macon County Court and he challenged E. P. Meador for the office of County Judge. Meador won.

Wash Patterson eventually relocated his family to Canton, Ohio, and later to Nashville, Tennessee. Patterson died on June 6, 1963 and his family had his body brought to the Smith Chapel Cemetery at Red Boiling Springs for burial.

The Dixon Embezzlement Trial

More that two years after Frank Dixon's indictment for embezzlement, his trial finally got underway. While he was under indictment on ten counts, the trial dealt with only one. The jury was to decide the matter of $8,546.21 Dixon allegedly embezzled from the county coffers.

Jury selection began on March 17, 1937 and concluded on the morning of March 19. Immediately after the empanelling of the jury, District Attorney John A, Mitchell began his case. Mitchell called three witnesses before Judge Chester K. Hart adjourned the court for the day.

On the second day of the trial, Saturday, March 20, the prosecutor resumed his case by calling Cager Archer of Red Boiling Springs; schoolteacher and former Chairman of the Macon County Court V. D. Bohanan; Tennessee State Auditor O. E. Hysmith; local merchant Witt Dillard; and Macon County Court Clerk Fred D. Gregory. After calling his witnesses, District Attorney General Mitchell rested his case. At that point, Judge Hart adjourned the court until Monday March 22.

Dixon, brought into the courtroom on a stretcher by attendants, had a top-notch legal team defending him. His attorneys included former Tennessee Governor Albert H. Roberts of Nashville, Thomas G. Henson of Lebanon, and J. M. Chamberlain of Lafayette. Dixon's team appeared confident of securing an acquittal.

When the trial resumed, Dixon's attorneys put on a defense that lasted only about fifteen minutes. Dr. Glenn Velia of the Madison Sanitarium testified that Dixon had been confined there for more than two years and that he was incapable mentally or physically of aiding in his own defense.

Then Dixon's attorneys called the Chairman of the Macon County Court, E. P. Meador. Meador testified that Dixon had repaid the county the $8,546.31 that went unaccounted for during his tenure. With that, the defense rested and Judge Hart ordered the jury sequestered while they deliberated.

On the morning of March 23, the jury returned to the courtroom and informed the judge that it was hopelessly deadlocked. Rumors were that ten favored acquittal and two desired a conviction. With no verdict possible from the jury, at 10:30 a.m. Judge Hart declared a mistrial. The hung jury effectively ended Dixon's legal problems.

Dixon experienced a complete physical and mental recovery and for the next several years, he remained in Lafayette and was active in the community. He even sought elective office again. In 1942, Dixon finished second to Grover West in a close race three-way contest for Macon County Judge.

Dixon died on March 7, 1981, at the age of 87. His burial place is Woodlawn Memorial Park and Mausoleum in Nashville.

Sources.

"Asks to Cancel Policy." *The Nashville Tennessean*, March 7, 1934, page 7.

Blankenship, Harold G. *History of Macon County, Tennessee.* Tompkinsville, Kentucky: Monroe County Press, 1986, pages 29, 153, 155-156.

"Cases of Former Officials Charged in Courthouse Fire Delayed Again." *The Nashville Tennessean*, November 20, 1935, page 18.

"Charged With Conspiracy in Connection With Fire." *Leaf-Chronicle* (Clarksville, Tennessee), November 20, 1935, page 4.

"County Races (Macon)." *The Nashville Tennessean*, August 6, 1932, page 5.

"Ex-Trustee Freed Of Arson Charges In Macon County." *The Nashville Tennessean*, November 22, 1935, page 1.

"Former Sheriff Dies." *The Nashville Tennessean*, March 1, 1935, page 21.

"Hotel Lincoln invites you to Red Boiling Springs." *The Nashville Tennessean*, July 9, 1933, page 16.

"Jury Disagrees in Dixon Case." *The Nashville Tennessean*, March 24, 1937, page 16.

"Jury in Dixon Case Locked Up." *The Nashville Tennessean*, March 23, 1937, page 6.

"Lawrenceburg Man Named GOP Manager." *The Nashville Tennessean*, August 12, 1948, page 3.

"Lost Records: Courthouse Fires and Disasters in Tennessee." Tennessee Secretary of State Website: https://sos.tn.gov/tsla/pages/lost-records-courthouse-fires-and-disasters-in-tennessee

"Macon Ex-Clerk Tried for Fraud." *The Nashville Tennessean*, March 20, 1937, page 1.

"Macon County v. Dixon." 20 Tenn. App. 425, 430 (Tenn. Ct. App. 1936).

"Scant Interest Seen In Primary." *The Nashville Tennessean*, August 8, 1937, page 22.

Scott, Betty C. Meadows. *Macon County, Tennessee Obituaries and Articles Volume 1*. Lafayette, Tennessee: Ridge Runner Publications and Genealogy Research, 2003, pages 27, 69, 89, 107, 121-123, 180.

"Services For Former Macon Trustee Are Held." *Macon County Times*, June 13, 1963. [Taken from a scrapbook of obituaries collected by Harold G. Blankenship.]

"State Rests Case In Dixon Trial." *The Nashville Tennessean*, March 21, 1937, page 10.

"Supreme Court Opinions." *The Nashville Tennessean*, July 15, 1934, page 5.

"Two Ex-Officials Of Macon County Indicted On Arson Charges." *The Nashville Tennessean*, March 27, 1935, page 1.

"Soldier Makes $10,000 Bond. *The Nashville Tennessean*, September 15, 1942, page 3.

"Votes Fair Fund." *The Nashville Tennessean*, August 6, 1935, page 3.

"West Takes Lead in Macon Race." *The Nashville Tennessean*, August 7, 1942, page 26.

57. Vance General Store Robbed

For many years, General Stores dotted the Macon County landscape. These stores sold most everything from plowshares to corsets. General stores served those living in close proximity to them who, for whatever reason, didn't want to "go to town" for groceries and other items. Many of general stores also served the same purpose as modern convenience stores. They sold gasoline, cigarettes, and snacks to passing motorists who were in a hurry to fill up and be on their way.

William Thomas "Will T." Vance ran a successful general store in Macon County's Eulia community. On March 3, 1933, Will T., following his usual routine, went to have lunch, leaving his 70-year-old father, Josephus "Joe" Vance, to watch the store.

While Will T. was away having his meal, two well-dressed men in a 1932 Chevrolet Coup bearing Indiana license places pulled up in front of the store and got out. One of the men was about 5'6". He donned a brown suit and a gray hat. The other one was about six inches taller than his companion was. The taller man wore a gray suit, a blue sweater, and a gray hat with a short brim.

The driver of the car purchased three gallons of gas, which in those days went for between 10¢ and 18¢ per gallon. He handed Joe Vance a $10 bill for his purchase of less than a $1. Joe told the men that he would have to go inside and get their change for them. The agreeable customers followed the elderly Vance into the store.

Will T. Vance kept a large amount of currency and business papers (checks, IOUs, etc.) in a leather billfold inside a showcase on one side of the store. Joe Vance removed the billfold, made change for the $10 bill, gave it to one of the men, and then put the billfold back from where he had taken it.

After Joe returned the billfold to the showcase, one of the men asked if the proprietor had any "Spark Plug" brand chewing tobacco. Joe said they didn't carry Spark Plug, but they had "Apple" brand chewing tobacco. The man said that Apple brand might do. The storekeeper and his customer went to the other side of the store to get the tobacco.

While the elder Vance was distracted with one man, the other grabbed the billfold from the showcase, shoved it into his pocket quickly, and then calmly sauntered outside. The thief passed Will T. Vance as the storeowner entered the building. Will T. did not sense that there was any problem.

The man inquiring about the tobacco, showing no signs of hurry, came out of the store, and climbed into the Chevy next to his partner. The robbers, acting as if they had not a care in the world, drove away in an easterly direction toward Lafayette.

It was m ore than an hour after the theft before Will T. discovered the billfold missing. By his estimate, it contained the substantial amount of $1,025 in cash, checks, and IOUs.

Will T. was certain that the two men from Indiana had taken the billfold.

Vance contacted Macon County Sheriff Virgil Brooks. Sheriff Brooks came to the store and took the descriptions of the men and their vehicle. He then alerted police and sheriff departments in the surrounding counties to be on the lookout for the robbers.

It had been more than two hours since the theft when the Sheriff informed the other law enforcement agents. This allowed the Indiana men to be as far as 100 miles away from the store before anyone outside of Macon County started looking for them.

There were few clues in the case. Word was that citizens in Westmoreland had seen the Chevy a short time before the robbery. Additionally, sometime after the robbery, road workers had spotted the getaway car as it passed them going at a rate of more than 50 miles per hour. Other than that, the trail was ice cold.

The robbers were only interested in the cash. They took out the money and then threw the billfold away leaving between $400 and $500 in checks and IOUs inside. The good news was that a traveling salesman found the discarded billfold lying in the highway about three miles from the store and returned it to Will T. Still, Vance suffered a hefty loss.

Sadly, Will T. Vance passed away less than three months after the robbery. He died of natural causes on May 28, 1933 at the age of 50.

Sources.

Blankenship, Harold G. *History of Macon County, Tennessee*. Tompkinsville, Kentucky: Monroe County Press, 1986, page 155.

"Macon Merchant Robbed of $1,025 But Recovers $400." *The Nashville Tennessean*, March 5, 1933, pages 1-2.

Scott, Betty C. Meadows, *Macon County, Tennessee Obituaries and Articles Volume 1*. Lafayette, Tennessee: Ridge Runner Publications and Genealogy Research, 2003, page 48.

58. Man Killed With Hoe

Sometimes, in the throes of a violent struggle, people cross the line, grab a weapon – any weapon – and lash out. Naturally, when that happens, tragedy often follows.

Chapter 41 described the death of Homer Davis at the hands of Deputy Sheriff Sam Hance in 1919. About fourteen years later, Homer's brother died violently as well.

Kermit Davis lived in Clay County. He was 24 and he made his living through farming. Money was tight in those days and disputes over even small amounts could lead to violent confrontations. Adding alcohol to the mix made violence even more likely.

On the afternoon of Sunday, April 4, 1933, Kermit Davis and Victor Bean were in a barn belonging to Bean's uncle, Claiborne Bean. Victor's cousin, Jim Bean was also in the barn.

Kermit and Victor had both been drinking heavily and they got into an argument over changing a $10 bill. Jim tried to calm things down, but the other two men continued to argue and a fistfight ensued. The fight escalated until Victor Bean grabbed a garden hoe and struck Kermit Davis over the right ear with it. The force of the blow fractured the victim's skull.

Friends transported Davis to his brother's home near Red Boiling Springs. Dr. H. C. Hesson treated the injured man, but he could not save him. Davis died on April 6.

Authorities issued an arrest warrant for Victor Bean charging him with first-degree murder. Before he surrendered, Bean told his wife he acted in self-defense.

On April 10, Bean went before Justice of the Peace Jacob Jenkins at Hermitage Springs. Jenkins awarded Bean bond and bound him over for trial.

Renovations to the Clay County Courthouse and other factors caused delays in the Bean trial for more than a year. He finally went before the court on May 7, 1934. A jury found him guilty of manslaughter and sentenced him to two years in jail.

Unwilling to accept his sentence, Bean filed an appeal. The judge continued Bean's bail while the case worked its way through the justice system. On January 12, 1935, the Tennessee Supreme Court affirmed the verdict and ordered Bean to prison.

In his continuing effort to get free, Bean requested a pardon from Governor Hill McAlister. After considering the appeal, Governor McAlister pardoned Bean on October 16, 1935.

Sources.

Blankenship, Harold G. *History of Macon County, Tennessee.* Tompkinsville, Kentucky: Monroe County Press, 1986, page 137.

Davis, Kermit. *Tennessee Death Records, 1908-1965.* Nashville, Tennessee: Tennessee State Library and Archives.

"Hearing to Be Monday." *The Nashville Tennessean*, April 9, 1933, page 2.

"Heavy Docket in Clay." *The Nashville Tennessean*, May 6, 1934, page 18.

"Held for Murder." *The Nashville Tennessean*, April 8, 1933, page 3.

Scott, Betty C. Meadows, *Macon County, Tennessee Obituaries and Articles Volume 1*. Lafayette, Tennessee: Ridge Runner Publications and Genealogy Research, 2003, page 53.

"Six Prisoners Pardoned." *The Nashville Tennessean*, October 17, 1935.

"Supreme Court Decisions Rendered." *The Nashville Tennessean*, January 13, 1935, page 6.

59. A Home Invasion

HOME invasions are not now, and have never been, common in Macon County. However, they have happened from time to time.

Lee Knight was 32. He lived on the Scottsville Road a few miles from Lafayette. In late April 1933, Knight's 28-year-old sister, Effie Jones was visiting him. A terrifying event ruined their pleasant evening.

Knight and Jones said that four armed men, without warning or provocation, broke into the house and robbed them of $1,000 ($400 in cash and $600 in notes).

Officer J. W. Maddox brought his fine collection of bloodhounds to Knight's house and put them on the trail of the robbers. The dogs led Maddox immediately to the home of Hubert Hire's father. Upon questioning, Hubert Hire confessed and he implicated his brother-in-law, Sam Graves of Old Hickory, Tennessee.

Sheriff Virgil Brooks and officer Maddox went to Old Hickory, located Graves, and arrested him. Upon their return to Lafayette, they locked the two hoodlums up together in jail.

A jury convicted Hire, Graves, and another man, Wes Lawson of the crime and sentenced them to prison terms. The alleged fourth robber escaped justice.

Sources.

"Two Are Held In $1,000 Robbery." *The Nashville Tennessean*, May 2, 1933, page 5.

"Prisoners Seek Release." *The Nashville Tennessean*, August 23, 1933, page 3.

"'Welcome Cowboy;' Macon County Jail Receives Fugitive." *The Nashville Tennessean*, November 3, 1933, page 2.

60. Glover Accuses Likens

IT is very difficult for members of law enforcement to do much without more to go on than the word of one person against another. Even if a police officer believes one person's word, the other person's statements carry just as much weight in a court of law. Because of the "one word is as good as another" principle, sometimes the guilty walk away free and other times the innocent face criminal charges.

On November 30, 1933, a shooting took place in Lafayette. Richard Glover suffered a shotgun wound to his hip. Fortunately, he survived the blast. Glover contacted the authorities and accused Dr. John Likens of shooting him.

Although there was no doubt that Glover suffered serious wounds, exactly how the shooting happened remained an unsettled question. Likens denied the charge, but Glover swore out a warrant and Sheriff Virgil Brooks felt duty bound had to act on it. He arrested Likens and brought him Justice of the Peace.

Again, there was no doubt about the fact that Glover was injured, but there was no evidence other than the conflicting statements of the accuser and the accused. Under those circumstances, Justices of the Peace usually dismissed all charges against suspects, but not this time. In this instance, the Justice placed Dr. Likens under a $1,000 bond and bound him over for trial.

Source.

"Lafayette." *The Nashville Tennessean*, December 2, 1933, page 6.

61. Murder on Gravel Hill

THE knowledge that one has money acts as a magnet to thieves. If the person with the money happens to be old or defenseless, he is even more attractive to criminals.

John Allen Carter was a hard working, 70-year-old African American farmer living in Macon County's Gravel Hill community. Those that knew Carter liked and respected him.

On February 3, 1935, Carter's son came up from Gallatin with some sweet potatoes and lespedeza grass seed for his father. When no one answered the door, Carter's son entered the house and found the old gentleman lying on the floor face up between two beds. Estimates made by the treating physician indicated that Carter had been dead for at least 48 hours when his son found him.

There was some physical evidence found on the scene. Carter's wife was not at home. She was visiting relatives in another community and apparently, he was preparing a meal for himself when the murderer or murderers came to his residence. There was blood on the floor at the front door of the Carter home indicating he died there and his assailants had dragged him to the place where his son found him. Additionally, investigators found a spent 16-gauge shotgun shell on the ground a few feet from Carter's front door.

Dr. I. L. Roark examined Carter and found that the victim absorbed a shotgun blast in the back below his left armpit. The pellets ranged downward, killing Carter.

The murder outraged Carter's many friends and neighbors and they demanded immediate action. They needed not to worry. Macon County authorities were determined to find the killer or killers as quickly as possible. A Justice of the Peace named Linville and a man named O. E. Bentle convened a Coroner's Jury. The jury members determined that Carter died at the hands of unknown parties.

Sheriff Jack Creasey began an investigation and soon found proof implicating a couple of suspects. The two were 24-year-old Hampton Jumper, and Gleason Adams (sometimes referred to as Adamson), also 24. Adams and Jumper were African Americans who lived in the Gravel Hill community not far from the Carter residence.

Creasey learned that John Allen Carter sold his tobacco crop during the last week of January, but he did not deposit his earnings in a bank. Instead, he went to Vance's General Store in the Eulia Community and asked Joe Vance to keep part of the money for him. Vance agreed and gave Carter a "Due Bill" for a little more than $20. Later, according to witnesses, Carter showed the due bill and $7.50 in cash to several people.

On either January 30 or 31, 1935, Gleason Adams came to Vance's store with a letter purporting to be from Carter. The letter authorized Vance to pay Adams $20 and to let him have some sugar and a bag of flour. Adams explained that he sold Carter a hog and a mule in exchange for the due bill. Vance gave Adams the money and goods and then prepared a statement attesting to the balance remaining on the Due Bill.

On February 1, Adams returned to Vance's store in a car owned by a white man named Herod Prock. Hampton Jumper was in the vehicle with Adams. Adams purchased some gasoline and paid for it with what appeared to be the same $20 bill Vance had given him during their previous transaction.

The alleged deal between Adams and Carter seemed dubious at best, and it was enough to cause Sheriff Creasey to suspect Adams of murdering the old man. Additional suspicion attached to Jumper, not simply because he was with Adams, but because Jumper had faced charges a couple of years before for breaking into Carter's home.

Adams and Jumper had left the Gravel Hill community soon after the murder and authorities acted on reports that witnesses saw them in the Old Hickory area of Davidson County and elsewhere. After a few days of searching, the Davidson County Sheriff informed his counterpart in Macon County that he had failed to locate the suspects.

Sheriff Creasey saw no reason to chase after shadows. Instead, he employed the old adage, "Criminals always return to the scene of the crime." On February 5, Creasey went back to the Gravel Hill area, located the hiding place of the two suspects, arrested them, and lodged them in the county jail.

Gleason Adams had been in custody only a short while when he decided to confess and implicate Jumper and Prock. Adams claimed that he and Jumper kept a lookout while Prock went into Carter's house and committed the murder. Adams said that he and Jumper helped Prock move Carter's body to where the old man's son found it. Adams added that Prock took a pocketknife and some money from the victim's pockets. Adams told the Sheriff that his reward for his part in the crime was receiving Carter's pocketknife, while Prock kept the money.

Although the statement Adams gave him did not dovetail with the physical evidence or explain how Adams came in possession of the Due Bill, Sheriff Creasey acted on it. Creasey went to Prock's home at about 11 o'clock on the evening of February 5, took him into custody, and jailed him. The 30-year-old Prock denied any complicity in the robbery and killing.

Later, Adams had a change of heart. He recanted his first statement and confessed that he alone had committed the crime. He gave his motive as "trouble" he and Carter had had shortly before the attack. The conflicting statements did little to clarify the case.

The three accused men went before Justice of the Peace, S. F. Jones in Lafayette on February 8. Jones bound the case over and scheduled the three men for trial.

On March 21, the three accused men stood trial. The event attracted such interest that the courtroom filled quickly with spectators. In fact, bailiffs had to turn a large number of those wanting to enter the courtroom away.

A number of those denied access expressed frustration that the courtroom in the new courthouse was too small to accommodate everyone. The angry people left outside the courtroom blamed the Macon County Court for the lack of space. One said, "That damn County Court ought to learn some sense before they build another building." Another outraged citizen said that Macon County should elect its next County Court from the Sears, Roebuck catalogue.

As far as the trial, the judge accepted the second confession offered by Gleason Adams. The judge concluded that Adams had acted alone, and sentenced him to life in prison. The judge ruled that Hampton Jumper and Herod Prock were innocent and they went home free men.

Sources.

Carter, John Allen. *Tennessee Death Records, 1908-1965.* Nashville, Tennessee: Tennessee State Library and Archives.

"Farmer Held For Death of Negro." *The Nashville Tennessean*, February 7, 1935, page 4.

Scott, Betty C. Meadows, *Macon County, Tennessee Obituaries and Articles Volume 1.* Lafayette, Tennessee: *Ridge Runner Publications and Genealogy Research.* 2003, pages 86-87, 93, 96.

"Sentenced For Life." *The Nashville Tennessean*, March 23, 1935, pages 16.

62. Gypsies in Macon County?

Although unfair, some groups have bad reputations based on stereotypes that have grown up around them. Their reputations become even worse when persons pretending to be members of those groups commit criminal acts.

In March of 1935, a group of purported Gypsies was running confidence games in Macon County. The alleged Gypsy band consisted of at least seven men and four women working in two separate teams.

Two of the women conned a man named W. T. Meador in the Rocky Mound community. They promised Meador that they could cure his rheumatism by the use of massage. Their cure consisted of rubbing and stroking his shoulders and arms until his rheumatism abated. Of course, the women were not interested in relieving Meador of his arthritis; they were interested in relieving him of his money.

While the man was distracted, the women took two pocketbooks from his pants without his noticing it. It was only after the pair departed that Meador discovered one of his pocketbooks lying on the ground. When he checked, he learned that the pickpockets made off with $35 he had in one pocketbook and $130 he had in the other.

Although the confidence game the women worked on him had to embarrass Meador, he nonetheless called Macon County Sheriff Jack

Creasey immediately. Creasey and deputized former Sheriff, Ed Sanders, gave pursuit, but the con artists crossed over into Kentucky before the law officers could chase them down.

Creasey alerted Kentucky authorities to be on the lookout for the roving band of miscreants. Shortly thereafter, Kentucky police informed Creasey that they had stopped and detained a party of six males and two females about eight miles north of Bowling Green and that they had lodged them in the jail there.

Meador and Creasey went to Bowling Green and Meador identified the women who had "cured" and then robbed him. The Kentucky authorities released the criminals to Sheriff Creasey and he returned them the Lafayette and incarcerated them.

Meanwhile, John Dycus suffered a con job too. Two women he believed to be Gypsies had lifted his pocketbook, taken the $2 in cash and a $10 gold piece from it, then discarded it on the fireplace hearth in his living room. Dycus had the two women and their male companion arrested. Creasey put them in his suddenly Gypsy filled jail.

The accused robbers used their phone call to let their leader know they were in trouble and he hurried from Nashville to rectify the situation. No one wanted a public trial and the band's most polite leader offered to return everything his friends had taken and to pay all costs associated with the matter if Sheriff Creasey would release the thieves into his custody.

All the parties involved in the affair agreed to the generous deal offered by the leader of the thieving band and the Sheriff released the con artists from jail. The entire group climbed into their cars and prepared to return to their home base in Nashville. But before they departed, the group leader tried to set the record straight. He said they were not actually Gypsies, but Indians from Brazil.

Source.

Scott, Betty C. Meadows, *Macon County, Tennessee Obituaries and Articles Volume 1*. Lafayette, Tennessee: Ridge Runner Publications and Genealogy Research, 2003, page 93.

63. A Nighttime Burglary

LIKE all businesses of its type, the Bennett and Cook General Store in the Green Grove community of Macon stocked a large variety of items. A group of thieves decided they wanted a portion of those items, but they didn't want to pay for them.

While darkness still engulfed the early morning hours of March 13, 1935, burglars broke into the store, collected about $400 worth of merchandise, loaded it into a car, and drove away with it. Items the thieves made off with included dress goods, men's suits, shoes, slippers, hats, overalls, dresses, overcoats, shirts, underwear, a clock, three large bags of potatoes, a bag of sugar, a case of eggs, cheese, candy, and toiletry items.

When the storeowners opened the establishment, they discovered the robbery and called Macon County Sheriff Jack Creasey. Creasey quickly identified a young man named Claude Edens as a person of interest in the crime. Creasey arrested Edens, took the suspect to the Macon County jail, and questioned him.

Edens broke rather quickly and confessed that he had acted as lookout while Harry Clements, Nealie Cook, Alice Holland, and Bill Jackson broke into the store and brought the goods out. Apparently, Edens also told Creasey where the culprits had gone after the robbery.

Creasey contacted authorities in Davidson County and on March 16, he and Davidson County Deputy Sheriff, Frank McDonald, raided a house located at 410 Second Avenue South in Nashville. There, they found the four individuals Edens had implicated. Creasey and McDonald found all the items taken from the Bennett and Cook General Store, except for one of the 100-pound bags of potatoes. Creasey and McDonald also learned that the suspects had moved into the house the day after the robbery.

After some preliminary questions, Creasey transported the accused robbers back to Lafayette where he lodged them in the county jail. Alice Holland made bond, but the men did not.

The authorities gave the accused a speedy trial. On March 21, with Judge Harry Camp, presiding, a jury convicted Harvey Clements, Nealie Cook, Claude Edens, and Bill Jackson. Each of the men received a sentence of three years in the State Prison. Alice Holland avoided conviction.

More than a year after the four men went to prison, based on several requests, Governor Hill McAlister reconsidered the case. After accounting for everything, the Governor stated that thirteen months in jail was long enough to spend incarcerated for the burglary of a county store, especially since the storeowners recovered almost all of the pilfered merchandise. Additionally, Governor McAlister pointed out "trial officials" had recommended clemency and he felt he should honor that recommendation. On April 28, 1936, the

Governor commuted the sentences of Clements, Cook, Edens, and Jackson.

Sources.

"Four Arrested Here for Robbery in Green Grove." *The Nashville Tennessean*, March 17, 1935, page 28.

"Four Get Commutations." *The Nashville Tennessean*, April 29, 1936, page 2.

"4 Given Pen Terms For Store Robbery." *The Nashville Tennessean*, March 23, 1935, page 16.

Scott, Betty C. Meadows, Macon County, Tennessee Obituaries and Articles Volume 1. Lafayette, Tennessee: Ridge Runner Publications and Genealogy Research, 2003, pages 92-93.

"Store Robbed at Lafayette." *The Nashville Tennessean*, March 15, 1935, page 18.

64. An Accidental Shooting

An accident can still be a crime, provided it comes about through reckless behavior. This chapter illustrates such a criminal accident.

On the evening of April 13, 1935, 13-year-old Viola Moore, 27-year-old Owen Harrison, and 22-year-old Leland Franklin were together at a Scottsville, Kentucky residence.

Harrison, who was from Macon County, and Moore scuffled over a shotgun. Suddenly, the shotgun discharged and the blast struck the girl in the leg causing serious injury. A short time later, the Community Hospital of Glasgow, Kentucky received Moore as an emergency patient and doctors, working with great skill, were able to save the child's leg.

Although there was no doubt that the shooting was an accident, law enforcement personnel arrested Harrison on the spot and charged him with assault and battery. Franklin hurried away to Nashville before the police could question him, but they later picked him up and transported him back to Kentucky.

Harrison and Franklin stood trial in Scottsville on April 24 for the shooting of Moore. After the short trial in which the accused could not dispute the evidence, the court determined both men responsible for the serious injuries the girl suffered. However, the court ruled that their degree of their culpability differed. Owen Harrison received a sentence of 50 days in the Allen County jail, and the court fined Leland Franklin $20 and ordered him to pay all court costs.

Sources.

"Girl 13, Accidently Shot; Tennessean Held." *The Nashville Tennessean*, April 15, 1935, page 12.

"Two Convicted." *The Nashville Tennessean*, April 25, 1935, page 5.

65. Burglars Rob Store

It doesn't take a degree in criminology to know that businesses with the most to steal are also the most likely targets of criminals. This is especially true of those establishments robbed after closing time by burglars.

Lafayette's West & Johnson Dry Goods Store was large, very well stocked, and it did good business. Naturally, it was only a matter of time before the establishment became the target of thieves.

Sometime in the early morning hours of October 18, 1935 robbers employed a pry bar to "jimmy" open the backdoor of the store. After getting inside, the burglars absconded with about $600 worth of dry goods, shoes, and other merchandise. Beyond what they took, the malicious criminals damaged many other items by throwing them on the floor and walking on them.

Investigators located the crowbar used in the crime and witnesses reported seeing a Roadster bearing Robertson County license plates with a flat tire stopped in the Hillsdale community. The witnesses said those with the car seemed "restless" as they added air to the flat tire.

Based on the information he had, the Macon County Sheriff called the Robertson County Sheriff's Department and requested that police officials be on the lookout for the suspects in the roadster.

The vigilance of Robertson County's law enforcement officials paid off. On October 21, they arrested two Springfield men, Robert Eskew and "Bully" Phelps (sometimes spelled "Phipps"). The suspects had some of the stolen items on their persons and police found other items belonging to West & Johnson at the homes of the accused.

Eskew and Phelps denied that they had stolen anything. They said they purchased the dry goods from a man named Louis Price. Upon searching Price's home, they found a large amount of the goods stolen from Lafayette in his attic. However, Price was not there. He had already fled the area.

In all, authorities only recovered about one-third of the goods taken from the West & Johnson store. Investigators in Robertson County surmised that the suspects in the case were part of a larger crime ring operating in Middle Tennessee. The Macon County Sheriff brought the two suspects back to Macon County and jailed them awaiting trial.

In late November of 1935, Judge Finis E. Harris presided over the trial of Eskew and Phelps. The jury convicted them and the judge ordered them to prison for three years each.

Source.

Scott, Betty C. Meadows, *Macon County, Tennessee Obituaries and Articles Volume 1*. Lafayette, Tennessee: Ridge Runner Publications and Genealogy Research, 2003, pages 115, 121, 123.

66. The Underwood Church Fire

In the 1930s, the vast majority of churches in Macon County were wooden structures. Additionally, because of the Great Depression, funds were always tight. This meant that insuring churches against fire was usually out of the question. When churches burned, the loss was usually total and rebuilding placed a great strain on congregations.

About 9 o'clock on the evening of Sunday, March 8, 1936, Ezra Perdue and some others discovered the Underwood Methodist Church on fire. Perdue and his friends could not save the uninsured building. The estimated loss was $2,000.

The blaze originated on the southern side of the church and it was suspicious because there had been no fire built in the building during that morning's services. The citizens of the Underwood community felt that arson was the likely cause of the blaze.

Suspicion fell quickly upon Joe Yokley and an Allen County, Kentucky schoolboy named Hooper Blankenship. Believing Yokley and Blankenship guilty of arson, B. P. Butrum and Tom Law swore out warrants against the pair.

Kentucky law enforcement officials located and arrested Yokley and Blankenship and held them until Sheriff Jack Creasey and Constable E. O. Sanders could come and pick them up. After taking possession of the suspects, the

Sheriff returned them to Macon County where Yokley and Blankenship made bonds of $1,000 each.

Justice of the Peace C. G. Dillard presided over a preliminary hearing for the suspects on Saturday March 14. A large number of citizens of the Underwood community attended the hearing with the expectation that Dillard would bind Yokley and Blankenship over to the Grand Jury for possible indictment. They returned to Underwood disappointed.

The prosecutor had nothing connecting Yokley and Blankenship directly to the fire. He admitted to the Justice that he lacked the evidence to proceed and he asked that Dillard drop all charges against the suspects. Dillard complied and Yokley and Blankenship went home.

Source.

Scott, Betty C. Meadows, *Macon County, Tennessee Obituaries and Articles Volume 1*. Lafayette, Tennessee: Ridge Runner Publications and Genealogy Research, 2003, pages 148-150.

67. Rumrunners Shoot Sheriff

WITH the end of National Prohibition, the number of illegal liquor shipments captured in Macon County declined, but they did not stop altogether. In fact, the interdiction of illegal alcohol remained a big part of law enforcement in rural Tennessee in the 1930s.

At about 1 o'clock in the morning of April 26, 1936, Sheriff Jack Creasey almost lost his life attempting to stop moonshine trafficking.

The story began on Jennings Creek Hill near the Willette community when Constable Hubert Tuck and Charlie West began pursuit of a car carrying two men and a load of whiskey. Unable to cut off the suspects, West stopped the chase car, and Tuck out got out. Tuck then went to call Sheriff Creasey who was at jail in Lafayette. Meanwhile, West continued to pursue the suspects' vehicle.

Constable Tuck telephoned Creasey and informed him of the "carload" of liquor headed toward Lafayette on the Red Boiling Springs Road. Tuck described the vehicle as a Ford Model-A Coupe. The Sheriff and the city night watchman, Tom Moss, armed themselves and stood by in anticipation of the bootleggers' arrival in Lafayette.

After several minutes of restless waiting, the Sheriff concluded that the Model-A had broken down on the highway. Creasey and Moss took the Sheriff's car and drove east along the Red

Boiling Road in search of the stranded bootleggers.

About two miles out of town, the officers encountered the Ford barreling toward them at a high rate of speed. Creasey attempted to block the highway with his patrol car and Moss got out, but he tripped and fell down.

As the bootleggers pulled their vehicle around the stopped police car, they fired at least three shots. Two bullets hit the Sheriff's car and another struck the Sheriff just above his left wrist. The bullet traveled up the Sheriff's forearm and exited just below his elbow. Sheriff Creasey and officer Moss returned fire, empting their pistols at the fleeing vehicle, but they failed to hit the shine runners.

Shortly after the exchange of gunfire, Charlie West shot past the Sheriff's car as he continued pursuing the speeding Ford. West caught up with his prey just as the outlaws entered onto Lafayette's Public Square. The Ford went to the right around the Square and West went to the left, cutting off the suspects at the entrance to Scottsville Road.

Perhaps luckily for West, after shooting the Sheriff, the bootleggers had thrown their weapon out of their car. Unarmed, they did not resist West and he arrested them. Almost immediately, Sheriff Creasey and officer Moss arrived and Creasey handcuffed the suspects. Inside the Ford, the Sheriff found several kegs containing a total of 35 gallons of liquor.

After placing the bootleggers in jail, Creasey consented to allow treatment of his wound by

Dr. D. D. Howser. Howser determined that the injury was not life threatening.

Upon questioning, the arrested men identified themselves as Raymond Rich and Jim Renfroe, both of Scottsville, Kentucky. Rich said he had a wife and two children. For his part, Renfroe said he had several motherless children. The pair told the Sheriff that they had borrowed the car in order to go to Gallatin for Renfroe's wedding. They denied they knew anything about the illicit alcohol in the vehicle. They also denied shooting at the Sheriff.

On April 26, Rich and Renfroe went before Justice of the Peace S. F. Jones. The men changed their story and admitted to possessing the liquor, but they still denied shooting Creasey. Jones set bond for the two accused men at $1,000 for each count. They couldn't make the bond and Sheriff Creasey lodged them in the county jail until the July term of the criminal court.

A jury convicted Rich and Renfroe on charges of possessing and transporting liquor and assault with the intent to commit first-degree murder. Considering the gravity of their crimes, the men received short prisons terms. The judge sentenced Rich and Renfroe to just three to five years each.

A Pay Hike for the Sheriff.

As this story and the one related in Chapter 44 illustrate, the job of Macon County Sheriff could be a very dangerous one. Interestingly, at the time the criminals shot Creasey, the Sheriff of Macon County did not receive a regular salary for his services. He did collect commissions and fees, and he did get free room and board in an apartment provided for him and his family at the jail. But he did not receive a steady paycheck.

That changed in 1937. State Senator Merlin West, who was from Macon County, proposed legislation to help the Macon County Sheriff. West's bill proposed to pay the Macon County Sheriff $60 per month plus those payments they already received.

The legislature passed the bill on January 21, 1937 and the Governor Gordon Browning signed it a week later.

The $720 yearly salary spike made the Sheriff's job a little more attractive, if not exactly lucrative. Even after the raise, the Sheriff remained one of the lowest paid county officials.

Sources.

Gammon, CL. *Revenue Raiders: Macon County's Whiskey War.* Lafayette, Tennessee: Deep Read Press, 2022, pages 106-107.

Private Acts of the State of Tennessee Passed by the Seventieth General Assembly Regular Session, 1937 Volume I. Nashville: Printing Department of the Tennessee Industrial School, 1937, pages 265-266.

"Seven Clemency Pleas Receive Approval Of Parole Board." *The Nashville Tennessean*, January 5, 1938, page 9.

Scott, Betty C. Meadows. *Macon County, Tennessee Obituaries and Articles Volume 1*. Lafayette, Tennessee: Ridge Runner Publications and Genealogy Research. 2003, page 161.

"Two Men Held. *The Nashville Tennessean*, May 1, 1936, page 32.

68. Liquor Raids Continue

VACATIONS were rare for Macon County Sheriffs in years past. The lack of deputies and resources made extended periods away from the job impossible.

Less than a month after bootleggers wounded him, Sheriff Creasey was back at work leading raids on illicit liquor operations in Macon County.

On May 21, 1936, Sheriff Creasey and Deputies O. E. Bentle, Ed Sanders, Henry Williamson, and G. I. Wooten raided three illegal distilleries and confiscated 1,100 gallons of beer and 12 gallons of newly manufactured moonshine whiskey. The officers also captured two large copper stills and arrested four moonshiners.

The first raid took place in Macon's Fourth District and netted 300 gallons of beer and two and one-half gallons of whiskey. The operators of the facility evaded arrest.

The second raid was in the Macon County's Fifth District. The Sheriff arrested R. L. Price and his son, Buddy and confiscated 500 gallons of beer, five and one-half gallons of newly distilled liquor, and found a shiny new 50-gallon copper still. Justice of the Peace Carl White set bond for Price and his son at $500 each.

The third raid also took place in the Fifth District. Macon County officers found 300 gallons of beer, four gallons of moonshine, and a 50-gallon still. The county officers arrested Nathan Blankenship and his son Galen during the raid. Justice of the Peace S. F. Jones set bond for the two men at $250 each.

Sources.

Gammon, CL. *Revenue Raiders: Macon County's Whiskey War*. Lafayette, Tennessee: Deep Read Press, 2022, pages 111-112.

"4 Arrested in Liquor Raids." *The Nashville Tennessean*, May 22, 1936, page 9.

69. Gangsters in Macon County?

DEPRESSION era desperados and gangland criminals captured the imagination of the American public. The reputations of these murderous outlaws were overblown and some rose to celebrity status. These criminals were not Hollywood creations, they were real, and they were very dangerous. Additionally, petty criminals emulated people like John Dillinger, "Pretty Boy" Floyd, Bonnie and Clyde, and other of the gangsters glorified as modern-day Robin Hoods by naïve citizens.

Gangsters may have passed through Macon County on Saturday October 3, 1936. That evening, Virgil Law of the Long Creek community was driving along in his 1933 Chevy in the Pleasant Hill area. About five miles north of Lafayette, two men in a big blue Packard sedan came up behind Law's car, passed it, blocked the road, and forced it to stop. Law noticed the back glass of the Packard was broken out. He surmised, wrongly, as it turned out, that the criminals had broken the glass to make it easier for them to shoot at pursuing police cars.

One of the men, brandishing a .45-caliber pistol, left the Packard, came up to Law's car, and got in on the passenger side. The man pushed the cold steel pistol barrel against Law's ribs and ordered him to drive off the main road. Frightened, Law complied.

When the car was between the Pleasant Hill Church and the schoolhouse beside it, the man ordered Law to stop. The Packard, which was following close behind, also stopped, and the man driving it got out. He also had a .45-caliber pistol.

Law observed the hoodlums. The one in charge was large. He weighed about 200 pounds and he was very muscular. He was dressed well. He wore a dark suit and a light brown hat. The other well-dressed man was smaller. He weighed about 160 pounds. The small was nervous and talkative.

The outlaws searched Law, but they were not very good at it. Law, a successful merchant, had managed to slip his wallet underneath is belt and it went undiscovered. The robbers found nothing more than 15¢ in one of Law's pants pockets. The crooks took it.

About this time, two unsuspecting hunters, Phillip Dyer and Clarence Walton came upon the scene. One of the thieves drew a double-barreled shotgun and ordered the hunters to stop and drop their weapons. They then searched Dyer and Walton. They found nothing on the hunters.

With the search complete, the robbers ordered one of the hunters to hold a lantern while the smaller outlaw removed the Illinois license plates from the Packard and put them and several other plates into the back seat of Law's car. Then, the hold-up men took four or five heavy suitcases from the Packard and put them in the Chevy. Law believed one of the suitcases held a machine gun.

The robbers told Walton that they were taking him hostage, but they would release him when they were sure they had crossed the Kentucky state line. Clarence Walton was rightly frightened. He pleaded with the hold-up men not to take him with them. He told the culprits that his wife was sick and that he was a poor man. Surprisingly, Walton convinced the outlaws not to take him. The smaller of the two even gave Walton a $1 bill to help with his financial problems.

As the outlaws were preparing to leave, the smaller man warned Law not to make any phone calls or to move the Packard. The criminal said he would return and kill Law if he disobeyed orders. Then, the criminal bragged that he and his partner had some trouble in Glasgow, Kentucky earlier in the day and that Law could read about it in the newspapers.

Finally, with the bragging finished, the two outlaws sped away in Law's auto. Instead of heading for Kentucky as they said they intended to do, they travelled toward Lafayette.

The event in Glasgow the little outlaw mentioned did take place. The two bandits had tried to hold up a car there, but had failed. The police had chased them, and fired several shots into the Packard breaking out the car's back glass. Thus, the two robbery attempts that day had left the incompetent crooks with 85¢ less than they started with.

When Macon County Sheriff Jack Creasey learned of the holdup, he sped toward Red Boiling Springs thinking the desperados would head that way. He was correct, they did pass through Red Boiling Springs, but Creasey didn't catch them. There had been some confusion in the robbery report, and Creasey was looking for the blue Packard sedan, not Law's Chevy.

The other law enforcement agencies in the hunt also had bad information and the robbers got away.

Source.

Scott, Betty C. Meadows, *Macon County, Tennessee Obituaries and Articles Volume 1*. Lafayette, Tennessee: Ridge Runner Publications and Genealogy Research, 2003, pages 183-184, 186.

70. Another Whiskey Bust

DISTRIBUTION of illegal whiskey in rural America remained a lucrative enterprise for decades. Those transporting "white lightning" gained a mythical status, especially in the southern United States. Always portrayed as heroic, young, good-looking, and driving fast cars, the rumrunners captured the imagination of many. Yet, as with all myths, this one was largely inaccurate. Most of the moonshine transports were not fast cars, but big trucks. And most of the drivers were not teenagers with packs of cigarettes rolled up in their tee-shirt sleeves, but middle-aged men that had intimate knowledge of their routes.

About 2 o'clock on the morning of March 13, 1937, Sheriff Creasey and Sumner County Deputy Ollie Gregory made a big haul. The stopped a truck on the road atop of Long Hungry Hill. The two men inside the truck identified themselves as Richard Abernathy and Thomas Robinson. Both men resided in Louisville, Kentucky.

Upon searching the truck, the officers found containers containing some 70 gallons of bootleg whiskey. The sheriff and his deputies destroyed 65 gallons of the whiskey and saved the other 5 gallons as evidence. Sheriff Creasey then arrested Abernathy and Robinson, took them to Lafayette, and locked them in the county jail.

Sources.

Gammon, CL. *Revenue Raiders: Macon County's Whiskey War.* Lafayette, Tennessee: Deep Read Press, 2022, pages 112-113.

Scott, Betty C. Meadows. Macon County, Tennessee Obituaries and Articles Volume 2. Lafayette, Tennessee: Ridge Runner Publications and Genealogy Research, 2003, page 15.

71. Civil War Veteran Robbed

THE elderly are always prime targets of the unscrupulous. If an elderly person has a large sum of cash, strong-armed robbers are very likely to attempt to get it.

Ransom Dillard served in the Union Army during the Civil War. He survived the war and settled on a farm near the Tennessee-Kentucky line about ten miles north of Lafayette. On Friday morning, April 2, 1937, the spry 90-year-old Dillard decided to go out to his cornfield and do a little work. He carried a hoe and a walking cane with him.

Soon after his arrival at the cornfield, two men, one of them wearing a mask, came upon Dillard. The hoodlums threatened to shoot the old man if he didn't give them all the money he had on his person. When Dillard attempted to put up a fight, one of the robbers knocked him down and took the small purse the old man kept in his left back pocket.

As was usual in those days, the elderly man kept most of his money with him at all times. The thieves made off with $202 of Dillard's life savings (one $100 bill, two $50 dollar bills, and two $1 bills).

At least one of the criminals had to be acquainted with Dillard. The robbers knew when he would be in his cornfield that morning, and they knew exactly which pocket held his purse.

The authorities brought in bloodhounds and they picked up a scent. The dogs led law enforcement to a house about a mile away from the assault, but it contained no evidence and there were no arrests.

Dillard suffered a cut to the back of his hand, and a few minor bruises, but he was strong and he recovered quickly. In fact, he lived for almost another decade. Dillard died on November 30, 1946, less than two months short of his 100th birthday.

Sources.

Dillard, Ransom. Commonwealth of Kentucky Department of Health, Bureau of Vital Statistics.

Scott, Betty C. Meadows, *Macon County, Tennessee Obituaries and Articles Volume 2*. Lafayette, Tennessee: Ridge Runner Publications and Genealogy Research, 2003, page 19.

72. Doctor's Residence Bombed

VIOLENCE against others takes many forms. Sometimes, people resort to bombs to attack their enemies. Such was the case in Red Boiling Springs in 1937.

Dr. R. A. Leslie was a "masseur." He moved to Red Boiling Springs around 1917 and had lived there for about two decades. Leslie was school trained in the field of mechanotherapy, which is the treatment of disease by manual, physical, or mechanical means. Chiropractors and sports medicine doctors employ some types of mechanotherapy extensively today.

Considered a pioneer in his field, Dr. Leslie specialized in treating patients by the use of massage and mineral baths. He did good business in the summer months when visitors flocked to the resort at Red Boiling Springs and took advantage of his services. He usually closed his bathhouse during the offseason when business at the resort was slow.

Dr. Leslie, it seems, had at least one violent enemy. On the evening of April 14, 1937, a powerful explosion occurred at the Leslie home. Investigation revealed that someone placed a strong explosive (either dynamite or a homemade bomb) under Leslie's back porch. When the device exploded, it blew the porch to bits and caused severe damage to the back of the building. Inside the house, the walls were "torn loose" and the steam pipes suffered extensive damage. Parts of the bathhouse connected to the main building were so badly devastated that Leslie deemed them a total loss.

It is possible that the bomber did not intend physical harm to Dr. Leslie or his family. The bomber may have been aware that Dr. Leslie was in Michigan, his wife was in Florida, and their daughter was away in school. If that was true, the bomber meant to destroy the doctor's business and nothing more.

Sources.

"Mechanotherapy." in *Merriam-Webster.com Medical Dictionary*, https://www.merriam-webster.com/medical/mechanotherapy.

Scott, Betty C. Meadows, *Macon County, Tennessee Obituaries and Articles Volume 2*. Lafayette, Tennessee: Ridge Runner Publications and Genealogy Research, 2003, pages 21-22.

73. Christmas Eve Murder

For most of us, the Christmas holiday season is a joyous time. Sadly, it is not the case for some. Occasionally, black hearted people use Christmas as a cover for murder.

James D. "Jimmie" Nixon was a 45-year-old farmer living in Red Boiling Springs with his wife Essie. On Christmas Eve 1937, Jimmie suddenly went into convulsions and he died a short time later. The examining doctor could not ascertain a direct cause for the man's affliction. However, the doctor did not suspect anything beyond natural causes in Nixon's death.

Although there was no solid evidence to indicate foul play, rumors of murder swirled around Nixon's death. Pressure from those wishing a closer investigation grew for almost a year. Finally, in November 1938, Tennessee officials ordered Nixon's body exhumed and some of his vital organs sent to Nashville for examination. Chemists in Nashville found large enough quantities of poison in Nixon's liver to have caused his death.

Suspicion fell upon Hurston King and the Sheriff jailed him. After King had been in jail for several months, on March 20, 1939, a Macon County Grand Jury indicted him for culpability in Nixon's death.

Perhaps hoping he could make a deal and get a lighter sentence, two days after his indictment, King confessed to his involvement in the killing. He then implicated Nixon's wife, Essie.

King stated that he purchased a quantity of strychnine and delivered it to Essie. She then administered it to Jimmie, killing him. With King's statement in hand, Sheriff Creasey procured a warrant charging Essie with first-degree murder. He then arrested her and lodged her in jail.

Essie Nixon and Hurston King went on trial in middle of July 1939. Large crowds squeezed into the courtroom every day of the weeklong proceeding and they witnessed, "One of the hardest suits ever held in the county." The attorneys delivered their closing arguments July 24 and after deliberating for about two hours, the jury found King and Nixon guilty of second-degree murder.

Both King and Nixon requested the opportunity to appeal their convictions and Judge Holliday scheduled August 3, 1939 as the date for hearing the defense motions for new trials.

Holliday agreed to allow the defendants to be free on bond until their hearing. He set the bond for each at $5,000. Essie made her bond and went home. King could not make his and he remained in jail. At the hearing, the judge granted Essie an appeal.

Fearing that Essie would attempt to do away with the proceeds of Jimmie's insurance policy and other property, his mother, Sarah Nixon, filed suit in Chancery Court. The Chancellor enjoined Essie from using the funds until after her appeal hearing.

Essie appealed the Chancellor's ruling to the Tennessee Supreme Court and in early February 1940, the High Court affirmed the lower court opinion enjoining Essie from benefiting from the insurance policy or other exempt property until her appeal concluded.

Sources.

"Escheats Law Held Invalid." *The Nashville Tennessean*, February 4, 1940, page 31.

Nixon, James D. *Tennessee Death Records, 1908-1965.* Nashville, Tennessee: Tennessee State Library and Archives.

Scott, Betty C. Meadows, *Macon County, Tennessee Obituaries and Articles Volume 2.* Lafayette, Tennessee: Ridge Runner Publications and Genealogy Research, 2003, pages 55, 104, 113-114.

74. Man Killed With Stilt

MURDERS are always tragic, but some murders are also weird. Sometimes the choice of the murder weapon is strange. Other times the reason for the murder is ludicrous. The murder described in the following chapter included a strange murder weapon and an absurd motive for taking a human life.

Arthur Nash was a 38-year-old farmer living in the Frog Pond community of Macon County. Nash had a neighbor named Sam West, also 38. On the evening of March 10, 1938, Nash and West had a deadly altercation in which a child's toy became a murder weapon.

That evening Sheriff Jack Creasey answered a call about a deadly incident. The Sheriff hurried to the Nash residence and found Arthur Nash dead. The Sheriff took Sam West into custody and transported him to Lafayette. After making sure West received treatment for a scalp wound, the Sheriff lodged him in the county jail.

Under questioning, Sam West freely admitted killing Arthur Nash, but he claimed he acted in self-defense. West said that he and Nash got into a fistfight. During the fight, according to West, Nash drew a knife and came at him at him with it. West continued that Nash either cut him, or hit him in the head with the knife, causing the scalp wound mentioned above.

Arthur Nash's 14-year-old son, Freedom, contradicted most of West's story. The youngster said that Sam West had been hanging around the Arthur Nash's residence for most of the day. That afternoon at about 6:30 p.m., Arthur Nash came outside and West followed behind him. West was angry about a previous transaction and he demanded $1 he claimed Nash owed him.

When Nash refused to hand over the dollar, it enraged West. West noticed one of Freedom Nash's stilts on the ground. Blind with anger, West grabbed the stilt, swung it hard, and struck Arthur Nash behind the ear with it. The blow killed Nash instantly.

Freedom Nash said he picked up the other stilt and hit West in the head with it twice, knocking the killer down both times. Freedom contended that his striking West is what caused the scalp wound the killer suffered. Freedom continued that after he knocked West down the second time, the murderer arose and chased after the boy threatening to kill him too, but Freedom escaped.

Murdered for a dollar bill, Arthur Nash left a wife and five children behind him.

This is a strange case indeed. Even though a dollar bill was more valuable in 1939 than one is now, a dispute over a single dollar should not have caused anger enough to send a man to his grave. Additionally, the choice of a child's play thing as a murder weapon is about as weird as it gets.

Sources.

"Man is Killed; Neighbor is Jailed." *The Nashville Tennessean*, March 11, 1938, page 28.

Nash Arthur, *Tennessee Death Records, 1908-1965*. Nashville, Tennessee: Tennessee State Library and Archives.

Scott, Betty C. Meadows, *Macon County, Tennessee Obituaries and Articles Volume 2*. Lafayette, Tennessee: Ridge Runner Publications and Genealogy Research, 2003, page 68.

75. Gravel Hill Church Fire

GRAVEL Hill was for a century or so, one of Macon County's most vibrant communities. Free African Americans, believed to be of Portuguese heritage, settled in the area in the early 19th Century and over the years, the community sported a post office, schools, and several business enterprises.

The heart of the Gravel Hill community was the Baptist Church. Not only was it a place of worship, but it was a social center. Among other things, the church often hosted singing events that hundreds of people, black and white, from Macon County and surrounding areas attended.

On Monday, January 13, 1939, the Gravel Hill community absorbed a serious blow when the Baptist Church burned. The uninsured building suffered a complete loss with damages amounting to about $1,000.

Church elders felt certain the fire was due to arson and suspicion fell quickly upon two residents of the Gravel Hill community, Willie Jumper and Elzora Jenkins. Sheriff Jack Creasey employed a team of bloodhounds and trailed Jumper to the man's home. Under questioning, Jumper made three contradictory statements and Creasey arrested him.

Justices of the Peace, J. A. Bandy and L. W. Thomas ordered Jumper bound over to the

Grand Jury and set his bond at $2,500. Jumper could not make bail and remained in jail.

There was no evidence against Jenkins and he was never charged.

Sources.

Blankenship, Harold G. *History of Macon County, Tennessee.* Tompkinsville, Kentucky: Monroe County Press, 1986, page 106.

"Macon Teachers Named for Year." *The Nashville Tennessean*, May 3, 1937, page 5.

Scott, Betty C. Meadows, *Macon County, Tennessee Obituaries and Articles Volume 1.* Lafayette, Tennessee: Ridge Runner Publications and Genealogy Research, 2003, page 169

Scott, Betty C. Meadows, *Macon County, Tennessee Obituaries and Articles Volume 2.* Lafayette, Tennessee: Ridge Runner Publications and Genealogy Research, 2003, page 97.

Conclusion

It is not the purpose of this book to imply that Macon County has ever been a notorious or exceedingly violent place. It isn't, and it never has been that way. The 75 stories relate events that really happened and they shed light on the Macon County of the era from which each of the stories came. They do not reflect on anyone not mentioned directly in these stories.

The hope of the author is that you enjoyed this book and that you learned a little about the history of Macon County in the process.

Acknowledgements

THE work of nonfiction authors would be extremely difficult, or even impossible, without the aid and research of others. It is only fitting that I mention some of those, living and dead, that aided directly, or indirectly, in this project.

The idea for this book came from several conversations about the Joe Cartwright case I had with Shelta McCarter Shrum. Beyond that, Shelta has provided me with many volumes of material on Macon County history that I relied upon heavily.

Harold G. Blankenship's *History of Macon County*, Tennessee was a valuable resource. Besides that, I referenced a scrapbook of obituaries Blankenship collected over a period of years.

Vickie Cherry graciously allowed me to use the drawing she did of the old Macon County Courthouse.

Judy M. Cothron edited several volumes of Macon County Censuses. They make the work of researchers easier.

Michael Meador answered some questions I had that indirectly aided in the production of this book.

John Oliver, the President of the Trousdale County, Tennessee Historical Society answered questions I had regarding some of the stories in this book.

Betty Scott's four Volume *Macon County, Tennessee Obituaries and Articles* is a terrific resource too.

June Shrum of the Macon County Historical Society took time away from her busy schedule to answer my questions and to help me locate some information I needed.

Finally, I'd like to thank Kim Gammon. Not only did she edit and do the cover art for this book, but also she has given me endless support for this and many other projects over the years. I am eternally grateful to her.

About the Author

CL Gammon has had a life-long fascination with the written word. This fascination has led to his authoring more than 60 books.

Gammon, who studied Political Science at Tennessee Technological University and History and Government at Hillsdale College, has received many prestigious honors including the Certificate of Appreciation for Service to the State of Tennessee, the Partisan Prohibition Historical Society Citation of Merit (the only two-time recipient), and nomination for the 2023 Gilder Lehrman Lincoln Prize.

Several universities, including the State University of New York and the University of Akron, have utilized his books as course material.

Articles written by Gammon have appeared in more than a dozen national and regional publications. He has also written feature articles for his hometown newspaper, *The Macon County Times*.

CL Gammon lives in Lafayette, Tennessee.

Index

Abernathy, Richard: 230

Adams, Gleason: 203-206

Akersville, Kentucky: 143

Allen County, Kentucky: 68, 144, 213, 217

Allen Hotel: 24

Allen, Lester: 175, 182

Allen, Wilson: 175

Andrews, A. H.: 142

Andrews, B. C.: 142

Andrews, Thomas: 97-99

Anglea, John: 66, 69

Archer, Cager: 186

Armstead, Fred: 115

Babbitt Metal: 158

Bandy, H. W.: 175

Bandy, J. A.: 242

Bank of Hermitage Springs: 152-156

Bate, Humphrey: 60

Bates, George: 73

Baxter, J. C.: 164

Bean, Claiborne: 195

Bean, Jim: 195

Bean, Victor: 195-196

Beasley, Isaac: 104-105

Beasley, Jerome: 71

Beasley, Pick: 70-74

Beasley, W. D.: 108

Bell, Julia: 84

Bennett and Cook General Store: 209-210

Bentle, O. E.: 203, 224

Bilbry, Marion: 146-147

Blankenship, Galen: 225

Blankenship, Hooper: 217-218

Blankenship, Nathan: 225

Blankenship, William W. "Bill": 184

Bloodhounds: 154-155, 171, 198, 233, 242

Bohanan, V. D.: 177, 181, 184, 186

Bowling Green, Kentucky: 159, 166, 207

Bowman, John: 113-116

Bradley, John: 35

Brawner, Bratton: 180

Brooks, Virgil: 144, 146-147, 149-150, 159, 162, 172, 175, 193, 198, 200

Browning, Gordon: 222

Browning, I. R.: 154
Burrow, Bud: 44
Burrow, Dero: 76-77
Burrow, William: 64, 95
Butler's Landing: 47
Camp, Harry: 178, 210
Canoe Branch: 62,
Carter, John Allen: 86
Carter, W. H.: 201-204
Carthage, Tennessee: 43, 72, 100-101
Cartwright, Enoch "E. G.": 17-19
Cartwright, John Wesley: 12
Cartwright, Joseph: 12-27
Cartwright, Martha Adeline *Brawner*: 12
Cartwright, Nancy: 17
Cartwright, Sarah W. *Smithwick*: 17, 19
Carver, Seth: 154-155
Carver, Sidney: 55-56
Castalian Springs: 59
Cedar Bluff: 141
Celina, Tennessee: 46-47, 154, 170
Chamberlain, B. V.: 176
Chamberlain, J. M.: 186
Chevrolet (Chevy): 162, 190-192, 225-226, 228
Chitwood, B. W.: 183-184
Chitwood, Harry H.: 180
Christmas: 57, 97, 116, 235
Citizen's Bank: 100
Claiborne, Willie: 19
Clark, Donnie: 137
Clark, Edgar: 137
Clark, J. C.: 37
Clarksville, Tennessee: 41
Clay County Courthouse: 195
Clay County, Tennessee: 132, 152-154, 194-195
Clements, Harry: 209-211
Cleveland, R. H.: 71-73
Clouse, Wynne F.: 177, 180, 182-183
Cloyd, H. J.: 46-47
Colter, Sam: 137
Communist(s): 119-123
Cook, Alice: 163
Cook, Nealie: 209-211
Cook, Oakley: 163
Cookeville, Tennessee: 178
Coolidge, Calvin: 123
Cothron, Billy: 45
Cothron, Lambert: 43-44
Cothron, Lloyd: 179
Cowan, H. C.: 67

Creasey, John "Jack": 209-210, 216, 218-221, 223, 227-229, 236

Crook, Henry: 63-64, 94-95

Cumberland River: 60-61

Curran, Henry: 80-82

Davidson Brothers: 146-147

Davidson County, Tennessee: 25, 81, 93, 108, 116, 121-123, 204, 211

Davis, Homer: 131-132, 194

Davis, Kermit: 194-195

Deaderick, James W.: 23-24

Dean, Albert: 99-102

Dean, B. M.: 100

Decker, Thomas: 97-98

Delirium tremens, (*DTs*): 18

Demijohn: 11-12

Diaz, Arnez: 23

Dillard, C. G.: 217

Dillard, C. H.: 176

Dillard, Ransom: 231-232

Dillard, Whitt: 185

Dixon, Franklin Pierce "Frank": 176-181, 185-187

Dixon, George: 65-66

Donoho, B. B.: 141

Donoho, William "Bill": 168-169

Doss, C. G.: 166, 179

Draper's Crossroads: 137

Duncan, Herschel: 88

Duncan, J. H.: 150

Durham, W. M.: 50, 56

Dycus, John: 207

Dyer, Homer: 103-104

Dyer, Phillip: 226

Easter: 150

Ebenezer: 45

Edens, Claude: 209-211

Electric Chair: 116

Elmira New York (Federal Reform School for Boys): 47

England: 122

Epperson Springs: 49

Eskew, Robert: 215

Espionage Act of 1917: 120-121

Essex: 162

Eulia: 37, 49, 55, 190, 202

Evans, Fred: 143

Fairview: 163

Farmers and Merchants Bank & Trust: 177

Fifth Amendment: 183

Flynn, James: 63

Ford (automobile): 162, 218-219

Ford, W. H.: 179

Foust, Ed: 101
Foust, J. E.: 64
Foust, T. E.: 64
Franklin, Leland: 212-213
Freeman, M. B.: 113-114
Freeman, Taft: 148
Frets, Jim: 83
Frog Pond: 238
Frye, Florence: 141
Frye, Virgil: 139-142
Gainesboro, Tennessee: 156
Gallatin, Tennessee: 37, 60, 63, 175, 201, 220
Gammon, Miller: 37
Gann, Jeff: 94
Gann, Lonzo: 105-109
Gann, Ottis: 150-151
Gann, Pattie: 94
Gap of the Ridge: 165
Gardenhire, Joseph M.: 96, 101, 106-108, 115-116
Gass, Bertle: 80-82
George DeHaven's Show (DeHaven's Imperial Circus): 39
Gibbs Crossroads: 136
Glasgow, Kentucky: 104, 145, 212, 227
Glover, Richard: 199
Goad, Earl: 139-142
Goad, Luelle: 127
Goad, W. C.: 64

Gold Reserve Act: 161
Goldfarb, Harry: 122
Gravel Hill (Hughes): 77, 201-203. 241
Graves, Dr. G. Y.: 166
Graves, Dr. Lattie: 166
Graves, Sam: 197
Gray, W. T.: 16
Great Depression: 161, 216, 225
Green Grove: 209
Green Valley: 158
Gregory, Dr. G. Shell: 120-123
Gregory, Fred D.: 163, 185
Gregory, Ollie: 229
Gregory, Tilford: 141
Gregory, Yerby: 179
Gross, Bud: 49-50
Guild, John G.: 21
Gupton, William: 122-123
Gypsy (Gypsies): 206-208
Hammock, W. M.: 64
Hance, Sam: 131-133, 194
Hance, W. S.: 156
Hancock, J. F.: 141, 149
Hanes, Johnnie: 103, 113-114, 125, 127
Hanes, Lee: 179
Hargis, Walter: 171
Hargis, Wayne: 150

Harris, Finis E.: 178-179, 215
Harrison, Benjamin: 51
Harrison, Owen: 212
Hart, Chester K.: 185-186
Hartsville, Tennessee: 17, 22-23, 39, 64, 72, 75, 101, 105, 150, 175
Harwood, G. W.: 134-135
Henson, Thomas G.: 186
Hermitage Springs: 152, 195
Hesson, Dr. H. C.: 131, 194
Highland: 105
Hillsdale: 63, 79, 214
Hire, Hubert: 197
Hix, Willie: 125
Holland, Alice: 209-210
Holland, Granville: 166-167
Holland, Ray: 166-167
Holland, William "Willie": 165-167
Holliers, Gene: 156
Holmes, Oliver Wendell: 119
Home Defense League, Nashville: 120
Horton, Henry: 132
Hotel Lincoln: 178
House, Clay: 83
Howser, Dr. D. D.: 220
Hudson Creek: 156
Hudson, Dewey: 156
Hudson, Doyle: 168-169
Hunter's Point: 60
Hysmith, O. E.: 185
Jackson County, Tennessee: 156-157
Jackson, Bill: 209-211
Jenkins, Elsie: 136-137
Jenkins, Elzora: 241-242
Jenkins, Jacob: 195
Jennings Hill Creek:
Jent, Connie: 129
Johnson's Inn: 14-15, 18
Johnson, E. J.: 136
Johnson, J. O.: 136
Johnson, Mike: 83
Johnson, Wint: 168-169
Jones, Albert: 88-89
Jones, Charlie: 112-117
Jones, Chester: 158-159
Jones, Effie: 197
Jones, Emerson: 179
Jones, Harvey: 112-115
Jones, Jim: 79
Jones, S. F.: 204, 220-221
Jones, Sam: 112-115, 117
Jordan, Max: 111
Jumper, Hampton: 202-205
Jumper, Willie: 241-242
Keel, James: 60-62

Key, Baxter: 180
King, Dr. William E.: 99-101
King, Ernest: 159
King, Hurston: 235-236
King, James W.: 25
King, Theodore F.: 86
King, Thurston: 145-146
King, Vestal: 154-155
Kirby, Dr. Marlin Luther: 30
Kirby, W. B.: 179
Knapp, John: 77
Knight, Hubert: 169
Knight, Lee: 197
Lafayette Church of Christ,: 11, 23
Lafayette Public Square: 11, 14, 16, 99, 175-176, 219
Lafayette, Tennessee: 11-12, 14, 16-17, 25, 28, 30-31, 39, 50, 64, 69-70, 75, 85, 99-101, 104-105, 107, 114, 120-121, 127, 134-135, 137, 145, 157, 166, 169, 173-175, 178, 180-181, 186, 191, 197, 199, 204, 207, 210, 214-215, 218-219, 225, 227, 229, 231, 238
Law, Tom: 216
Law, Virgil: 225-228
Lawson, Wes: 197
Leath & Ward General Store: 170
Leath, J. W.: 141

Lee, W. V.: 101
Leslie, Dr. R. A.: 233-234
Ligon, L. A.: 101
Likens, Dr. John: 199
Long Creek: 225
Long Hungry: 229
Macon Bank & Trust: 12
Macon County Courthouse: 64, 96, 162, 166, 172-174, 176, 179-184, 205
Maddox, J. W.: 197
Madison, Tennessee: 179, 186
Marshall, J. C.: 64
Marshall, Jack (Major Wise): 65
Mason, Dick: 83
Massey, Malcolm: 156
Maxey, Marlin: 111
May Day: 121-122
McAlister, Hill: 195
McConnell, N. W.: 17, 19-22
McDonald, Frank: 210
McMurry & Hamilton law firm: 22
McNichols, Ernest: 60-62
Meador, E. P.: 184, 186
Meador, W. T.: 206-207
Meadors, Henry: 141
Meadows, Weldon: 152-154

Mechanotherapy: 233
Minnick, Frank: 68
Mitchell, John: 180, 182-183, 185
Monroe County, Kentucky: 103-104, 143
Montgomery County, Tennessee: 41
Moonshine (Moonshiners, "Wildcatters): 28-29, 34-36, 51, 90, 127-128, 136, 156, 218, 223, 229
Moore, Viola: 212
Morgan, Proctor: 154
Moss, Tom: 218-219
Murphy, W. J.: 69-70
Nash, Arthur: 138-239
Nash, Freedom: 239
Nashville, Tennessee: 47, 49, 59-60, 73, 80, 82, 92, 107-108, 114-116, 120, 122, 129, 134, 140, 176-177, 181-182, 185-187, 207-208, 210, 212, 235
New Haven, Connecticut: 47
Newberry, Bedford: 168
Nichols, Robert: 105
Nixon, Essie: 236-237
Nixon, James D. "Jimmy": 235-236
Nixon, Sarah: 236
Old Hickory, Tennessee: 197, 203
Oldsmobile: 134-135

Packard: 225-228
Parker, Arch: 105-106
Parker, Archie, B.: 105-109
Parker, Brink: 105-109
Parker, Monk: 105-107
Parker, Rom: 105-106, 108
Parker, Sam: 45
Parkerson, Alice: 49-50
Parkhurst, Cordell: 145-146
Parkhurst, Foble: 146
Patterson, Thomas: 55-56
Patterson, Washington C. "Wash": 174-175, 177-185
Peay, Austin: 108-109
Peyton's Creek: 70
Phelps, "Bully": 215
Phillips, J. M.: 28-30, 35-36
Pierson, Joe: 75-76
Piper, D. Henry: 175-176
Pleasant Hill: 225-226
Pleasant Shade: 71-72, 136
Plymouth: 162
Pontiac: 162
Porter Detective Agency: 60
Portuguese: 241
Price, Buddy: 223

Price, Louis: 215
Price, R. L.: 223
Prock, Herod: 203-205
Purcell, Willie: 179
Ragland, James: 92, 94-96, 100-101, 106
Ramsey, Ernest: 156
Raynes, Susie: 67
Red Boiling Springs, Tennessee: 28, 46, 69, 111, 127, 131, 134-136, 145-146, 153, 178, 183, 185, 194, 218, 227, 233, 235
Reece, Newt: 69
Reeves, Hat: 106
Renfroe, Jim: 220
Rich, Raymond: 220
Riddleton: 43
Roark, Dr. I. L.: 21-22, 64, 166-167, 201
Roberts, Albert H.: 117, 186
Robertson County, Tennessee: 214-215
Robinson, Thomas: 229
Rocky Mound: 206
Roosevelt, Franklin D.: 159
Rushton, J. T.: 116
Rye, Thomas C.: 108
Ryman Auditorium: 123
Salt Lick: 57, 81
Sanders, Buster: 165-167

Sanders, Edwin O. "Ed": 132, 134-135, 207, 216, 223
Sanders, Ethel: 167
Sanders, George: 165-167
Sanders, Hugh: 11-16, 18-23
Sanders, Jodie: 165-167
Sanders, Raymond: 165-167
Scott, Jim: 179
Scott, Russell: 122-123
Scottsville, Kentucky: 154, 166, 175, 212, 220
Seagraves, Henry: 28-29, 31-34
Sears, Roebuck Catalogue: 205
Selective Service Act: 120-121, 124
Siloam: 31
Smith Chapel: 185
Smith County Courthouse: 101
Smith County, Tennessee: 43, 67, 70-73, 100-101
Smith, Ben: 146
Smith, W. A.: 64
Smith, W. W.: 129
Smith, Will: 156
Snyder, Elijah: 46-47
Sparta, Tennessee: 178
Spear, Alex: 153-154

St. Mary Parish, Louisiana: 65

Stewart's General Store: 77

Stone, W. B.: 136-137

Strychnine: 236

Sullivan, J. E.: 170

Sullivan, Virgil: 179

Sumner County, Tennessee: 31, 33-34, 59-61, 67, 229

Sutton, James: 156

Swindle, Frank: 179

Swindle, Lloyd: 171

Taylor, Robert Love: 54, 73

Templeton, Alison: 77

Tennessee Supreme Court: 21-23, 107-108, 132-133, 177, 195, 237

Thomas, L. W.: 241

Tompkinsville, Kentucky: 143

Toronto, Canada: 107

Trousdale County, Tennessee: 39-40, 63-64, 67, 76, 88, 101, 151, 244

Tuck, Herman: 179

Tuck, Hubert: 156, 216, 218

Tuck, W. L.: 47

Turner, J. J.: 22

Turner, John: "Jack": 57

Turner, Louisa: 57

Underwood: 216-217

Union Telephone Company: 85-86

United States Constitution: 120

United States Supreme Court: 119

Vance General Store: 190, 202

Vance, Josephus "Joe": 190-191, 202-203

Vance, William Thomas "Will T.": 190-192

Vanderbilt University: 122-123

Vaughn, Albert: 158

Vaughn, Ted: 177-178

Velia, Dr. Glen: 186

Wallace, John: 31

Walnut Shade: 168

Walton, Clarence: 226-227

Warner, Louise: 184

Watertown, Tennessee: 108

Weatherford, Joseph R. "Joe": 50

Webb, Harley: 156

Webbtown: 170-171

West and Johnson Dry Goods Store: 214-215

West, Charlie: 218-219

West, Grover: 187

West, Joe: 174

West, Merlin A.: 180-181, 221

West, Sam: 238-239

Westmoreland (Coatstown), Tennessee: 37, 49-50, 67, 192

White, Carl: 223

White, Elisha: 41

White, James: 182

White, Josh: 148

White, Lassie May: 181-182, 184

White, Rosie: 148

White, Sam: 137

White's General Store: 143

Whittemore and Doss General Store: 166

Willette: 125, 127, 139, 168, 218

Williams, Joe: 177-178

Williams, R. C.: 72

Williamson, Henry: 223

Willis, James: 165-167

Wilson County, Tennessee: 60-61

Wilson, Woodrow: 119, 121

Wooten, G. I.: 223

Wooten, John S.: 101

World War I: 108, 119, 123, 125

Wright, W. H.: 53-54

Writ of *habeas corpus*: 65, 100-101

Yokley, J. L.: 136

Yokley, Joe: 216-217

www.ingramcontent.com/pod-product-compliance
Lightning Source LLC
Chambersburg PA
CBHW071656090426
42738CB00009B/1549